Endorsements

'Many people think that Christian faith requires an irrational leap in the dark. Bernard V Palmer helpfully deconstructs this myth and [...] s the objective and subjective evidence for trusting in [...] able, logically and compelling way. Drawing [...] al doctor and Christian apologist, he writes [...] e passion of a pastor. He engages with pl [...] exposes the weakness of common objection [...] ility of the biblical testimony to Jesus. Thi [...] people who are sceptical or investigating the Christian faith for themselves. It will also equip Christians to share their faith more effectively and to give the reasons for the wonderful hope they have.'

John Stevens,
National Director – Fellowship of Independent Evangelical Churches

"Stepping Stones to Faith" is a tour de force. Based on talks given at universities and in churches around the big question "Is the gospel true?", this is classic Bernard V Palmer. Drawing on sources as diverse as Richard Dawkins and Peanuts, he builds his case with characteristic urgency. He skillfully navigates a series of stepping stones, including the evidence from science, the validity of human values and the historicity of the Gospels. Each chapter stands on its own, but the impact of the whole is both cumulative and compelling. As you read, you will feel the pulse of a passionate evangelist who aches for his readers to see the truth and beauty of the Lord Jesus. This is an important book for seekers and sceptics, doubters and disciples. In an increasingly sceptical world, Bernard shows us that entrusting ourselves to Jesus is not a leap in the dark, but a step into the light.

Richard Underwood,
Pastoral Ministries Director, FIEC (retired)

Is there more to life? There certainly is, and this book will help the reader to find out what that is, in and through the person of Jesus Christ. Relevant, readable, reliable, and written in a lively style, I valued this book and will recommend it to others.

Dick Lucas,

Rector Emeritus, St Helen Bishopsgate

"Bernard's enthusiasm and passion shine through as each chapter takes you to another stepping stone on the path to faith. He is forthright and challenging as he tackles many obstacles people have to faith and sets them thinking. There is an expertise that comes from his own background and training but also from having thought through these issues for many years. Being both widely read and very readable makes this a great book to read and to lend."

Hugh Palmer,
Retired Rector, Langham Place

Bernard V Palmer has provided a readable, accessible survey of the best scientific and historical evidence—along with the best philosophical arguments—for belief in Jesus Christ as Creator, Lord, and Savior. A superb overview!

Hugh Ross,
Astrophysicist, Christian apologist, and founder of 'Reasons to Believe'

I've read this book and it's really good. I have forwarded a copy to a few men in the village.

Doug Richardson,
Retired Dental Orthodontist and Fellow of The World Federation of Orthodontists

I would like to say how eminently useful I've found the Stepping Stones metaphor in my own evangelism and preaching. It makes so much more sense to follow the evidence and take the small step of faith than to discount the evidence and take the giant leap back into unbelief.

Andy Palmer,
Senior Minister, Christ Church Balham

Steppg Stones begins by asking the question many (perhaps most) people in our western culture find themselves asking at times: 'Is there more to life?' Often, though, that question is quickly suppressed, because we have been conditioned to think all matters of 'faith' irrational, but also because the possible implications of such exploration are uncomfortable. Bernard V Palmer, a surgeon trained and tested in evidence-based realities, leads the reader's steps gently but firmly through science and logic to see that faith in the real God is indeed robustly rational, and that the implications of knowing him as revealed in Jesus Christ are not constricting, but wonderfully liberating. From the opening story of an imaginary conversation between twins in the womb you will be both charmed and hooked! I thought it was terrific.

William Philip,
Senior Minister, The Tron Church, Glasgow and former physician.

In a world of soundbites and superficial judgements, Bernard's book helpfully draws together many of the coherent reasons to explore the Christian faith as credible and reliable, in a way that will encourage people to think more deeply about faith in Jesus Christ. With his widely sourced and varied illustrative stories, this book will appeal both to those who are exploring Christianity and those who want to help explain it better to their friends.

Rt Rev Dr Rob Munro,
Bishop of Ebbsfleet

Bernard went from Bedford School to Downing College, Cambridge in 1963 where he read Natural Sciences. He was then awarded the Price open scholarship to the Royal London Medical School for clinical training. There he captained the tennis club as well as playing hockey and squash. He was fortunate to have both his preclinical houseman posts in his teaching hospital. He then took a year out to be the first student worker for St Helen's Bishopsgate with the Rev Dick Lucas.

He then undertook his surgical training in major London hospitals and took the exams both to be a physician and a general surgeon. He was a Senior Registrar at the Royal Marsden Hospital in London and during this time undertook research in tumour immunology at the Institute of Cancer Research. He wrote many medical papers. In 1983, he was appointed Consultant Surgeon at the Lister Hospital in Stevenage where he worked until he retired. He was a general surgeon with major interests in Surgical Oncology and Gastrointestinal Surgery.

He became a convinced Christian when an undergraduate in Cambridge and has been a Bible teacher since. He has been active in the Christian Medical Fellowship and was one of their Trustees for many years. He is the author of 'Cure for Life', which has been translated into many languages and is now in its 5th English edition. This book was originally written for his patients to try to answer their questions about the purpose of life but this book has since found a world-wide niche and has been translated into many languages. Other books include 'The Duty of a Disciple' and 'Science and God: Enemies or Allies'.

He was asked to help found Christchurch Baldock in 2000AD where he regularly teaches.

He is a popular speaker in universities and churches both at home and overseas. He has written widely on the evidence for the Christian faith and what being a Christian means. He is also an evangelistic Bible teacher. He was appointed to be a visiting Scholar by 'Reasons to Believe' in Los Angeles.

Bernard's wife, Rosy, retired from nursing when they had a family. They have four Christian children, Rob (a General Practitioner Doctor in North London) Sam, (a Design Manager), Rachel, (a doctor and mother, married to the Director of UFM, a missionary organization), and Andy, the Senior Minister of Christchurch Balham in London. Bernard and Rosy now have 14 grandchildren whom they love and long to teach tennis and table tennis to.

Bernard has a website, www.bvpalmer.com in which many of his articles, video interviews and books can be found.

This book is dedicated to my life partner and wife, Rosy. She is a constant inspiration to keep making living for the Lord Jesus my priority in life, and I owe her so much.

Bernard V Palmer

STEPPING STONES

To Faith

AUSTIN MACAULEY PUBLISHERS™
LONDON * CAMBRIDGE * NEW YORK * SHARJAH

Copyright © Bernard V Palmer 2024

The right of Bernard V Palmer to be identified as author of this work has been asserted by the author in accordance with sections 77 and 78 of the Copyright, Designs and Patents Act 1988.

All rights reserved. No part of this publication may be reproduced, stored in a retrieval system, or transmitted in any form or by any means, electronic, mechanical, photocopying, recording, or otherwise, without the prior permission of the publishers.

Any person who commits any unauthorised act in relation to this publication may be liable to criminal prosecution and civil claims for damages.

A CIP catalogue record for this title is available from the British Library.

ISBN 9781035815463 (Paperback)
ISBN 9781035815470 (ePub e-book)

www.austinmacauley.com

First Published 2024
Austin Macauley Publishers Ltd®
1 Canada Square
Canary Wharf
London
E14 5AA

There are so many who have helped me to think clearly about the meaning of life and where to find answers. I am so grateful for those leaders of Lymington holidays; a part of the Titus trust, where foundations were laid. Members of the Christian Union in Cambridge helped me understand the Bible better and give me a concern to share its message. In my early Christian life, teachers of the Round Church in Cambridge, Mark Ruston and David Watson helped me greatly. I am particularly grateful to Dick Lucas of St Helens Church Bishopsgate who has helped me immensely. Subsequently colleagues in the Christian Medical Fellowship and in the Reasons to Believe team in the United States, who appointed me a visiting scholar, have inspired me to continue to seek answers to the great questions of life. I now have the privilege of working with members of Christchurch Baldock in our ambition to share the gospel with others around us.

In particular, I would like to thank those many scholars teachers and friends who love the Lord Jesus, who love his word the Bible, and who recognise that God has given us minds to try and unify all fields of knowledge.

Table of Contents

Introduction	15
Chapter 1: Is There More to Life?	17
Chapter 2: Is There a God?	22
Chapter 3: Science	30
Chapter 4: What If There Is No God?	44
Chapter 5: The Validity of Values	55
Chapter 6: 'God Is, Therefore I Am'	59
Chapter 7: Contemporary Witnesses to Jesus	69
Chapter 8: Further Evidence Given by Jesus	76
Chapter 9: Old Testament Prophecies	86
Chapter 10: The Real Jesus	97
Chapter 11: Did Jesus Rise from the Dead?	106
Chapter 12: The Jesus of History	115
Chapter 13: Early Church Growth	127
Chapter 14: Instincts and Innate Values	131
Chapter 15: The God-Shaped Gap	142
Chapter 16: The Consequences of Rejecting God	146
Chapter 17: Can the Gospels Be Trusted?	152
Chapter 18: A Leap or Step of Faith?	168
Chapter 19: Why Is It So Hard to Change Your Mind?	172
Chapter 20: Experience and Reason	180
Chapter 21: 'How Can I Be Saved?'	190
Summary	199

Introduction

In the second century AD, there were several men who wrote 'apologias' or explanations that included evidence for the Christian faith. Many were addressed to the Emperors on behalf of Christians who were being persecuted.

Today 33% of young people and 9% of adults are unsure whether there is a God, 40% of adults and 46% of youngsters don't believe that Jesus was a real person. Many do not know the evidence for the historic Jesus and most have not understood the implications of such thinking. Hence there is a need for a new book to explain these facts and arguments to people.

Others say, "I cannot believe in God because science has disproved it!" It is now apparent that such reasoning is invalid, **modern science supports what the Bible teaches and the Bible supplies what science cannot.**

Richard Dawkins' has suggested in his book *The God Delusion* that religious faith is irrational. "Dyed-in-the-wool faith-heads are immune to argument."[1]

He thinks that faith is a 'process of non-thinking', which is 'evil precisely because it requires no justification and brooks no argument'. In contrast, Alister McGrath, the Andreas Idreos Professor of Science and Religion at the University of Oxford, has said,

"Belief in God is not irrational but possesses its own distinct and robust rationality. It represents a superb way of making sense of things."[2]

The reasons people accept certain ideas is often dependent on previous experiences. If you had a Religious Education teacher at school that you didn't like, it is likely that you will not only reject that person but also their beliefs. If a person enjoys living in a way that they know is contrary to what the Bible

---

[1] Richard Dawkins, The God Delusion (Boston and New York: Houghton Mifflin, 2006), p. 28.

[2] https://www.bethinking.org/does-science-disprove-god/isnt-science-more-rational-than-faith

advocates, whether sexual or social, then there will be pressures to reject the Bible's message.

Not only do people have emotional needs for God but we all have personal reasons why we want to reject him. If there is a God, he has the right to control how I should live. In a court of law, a judge is not permitted to become involved in any case in which he has an interest because it is inevitable that there would be some bias in his judgment. Yet there is clearly much bias in the decisions people make about the place given to God and Jesus in people's lives. The Bible teaches that we can 'suppress the truth' by our wickedness (Romans 1:18) and that, in God's eyes we are culpable for doing so. This book outlines the types of evidence that there is a real God who has revealed himself in the person of Jesus Christ.

Chapter 1
Is There More to Life?

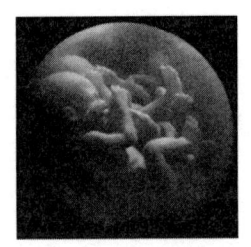

In a mother's womb were two babies. One asked the other: "Do you believe in life after delivery?"

The other replies: "Why? Of course. There has to be something after delivery. Maybe we are here to prepare ourselves for what we will be later."

"Nonsense," says the other. "There is no life after delivery. What would that life be?"

"I don't know but there will be more light than here. Maybe we will walk with our legs and eat through our mouths."

The other says, "This is absurd! Walking is impossible. And eat with our mouths? Ridiculous! The umbilical cord supplies nutrition. Life after delivery is to be excluded. The umbilical cord is too short."

"I think there is something and maybe it's different to life here."

The other replies, "No one has ever come back from there. Delivery is the end of life and in the after-delivery it is nothing but darkness and anxiety and it takes us nowhere."

"Well, I don't know," says the other, "but certainly we will see mother and she will take care of us."

"Mother? You believe in mother? Where is she now?"

"She is all around us. It is in her that we live. Without her there would not be this world."

"I don't see her, so it's logical that she doesn't exist."

To this the other replied, "Sometimes, when you are quiet, you can hear her, you can perceive her. I do believe that there is a reality after delivery and we are here to prepare ourselves for that reality."

Seeking God in our lives can at times seem illogical or impossible. We all know someone who will insist that there's no point in seeking God – the material world is all there is! But seeking answers, being curious about life and death, wanting the truth – these are all great human qualities and we must pursue them. There are those who think that religious people are living by blind faith whilst secular people base their position on scientific evidence and reason. I hope to show that the opposite is true. Secularism is also a belief system but it fails to account for many vital features of our existence.

How could the twins dilemma be resolved? There is the evidence from the developing organs such as hands, feet, eyes and ears that are there for a reason. Aren't our sense of values and purpose indicative that there is more to life than living for myself. The twins could hear their mother speaking and reassuring them – if they are willing to listen. We also have God's word given by his prophets and apostles. However the perfect way would be if someone from the outside world could enter the twins world and give a first-hand explanation about what life is really for. That is the Christian claim.

Stepping Stones

Imagine a river with its banks on either side. One bank represents a godless selfish world where everyone does their own thing, there is 'no king; everyone does as he sees fit.' [3] Hatred, dishonesty and selfishness are rife as each individual makes himself a king, resulting in fear, anxiety and loneliness. Governments swing between totalitarian control by dictators of either right or left or who, being of this world will also have their self-interest at heart and leave individuals behind. On the opposite bank is God's world where control is in the hands of a beneficent Lord. All its subjects are committed to living under His authority. What He wants happens but people are happy because he is a true God of love. In this kingdom, there is sharing, happiness and contentment.

Although there are many benefits of living in God's kingdom, it seems as if a giant leap of faith is required to jump across. As a rational being that leap seems

---

[3] Judges 21:25

to be large. But look, there are stepping stones across the river, each with a name written on it. Each stone represents a rational reason why it is right to live in God's kingdom. The stones are in groups. As any faith should be evidence based, the evidence represented by these stones is very important.

a. Science – evidence from science that there has to be a creator.
b. Logical deductions if there is no God.
c. The validity of values, love, honesty and integrity are real values.
d. The person of Jesus, his person, teaching, miracles and resurrection – his claims to be the Messiah.
e. Historical evidence for Jesus.
f. Old Testament prophecies about the Messiah.
g. The early church – why did it grow so quickly?
h. Our instincts for good – where do they come from?
i. The 'God-shaped gap' – why is it there?
j. The reliability of the written gospels – evidence that they can be relied upon.

Within each group of stones, there are many arguments and a book, such as this, can only summarise these. However all the arguments together make a very convincing case that there is indeed a God who has entered this world as Jesus Christ in order to save people so that they can become his representatives. It is by beginning with God that we can make sense of life.

What is knowledge?

The word 'science' comes from the Latin 'scientia', which meant 'knowledge'. All true knowledge has to be substantiated by evidence and reason. This is so for every area of life, including theological matters. Theology used to be called the Queen of Sciences as it was considered the supreme discipline, encompassing all other aspects of knowledge which were ratified by the God who created us and had revealed Himself to us. The greatest problem with religion has been when people have followed so-called prophets or religious leaders without a thorough investigation of their claims. The atheist Richard Dawkins was right in one respect when he wrote an open letter to his daughter Juliet. He laudably encouraged her to think for herself:

"Next time somebody tells you something that sounds important, think to yourself: "Is this the kind of thing that people probably know because of evidence? Or is it the kind of thing that people only believe because of tradition, authority or revelation?" And next time somebody tells you that something is true, why not say to them: "What kind of evidence is there for that?" And if they can't give you a good answer, I hope you'll think very carefully before you believe a word they say."

True knowledge and this must include answers to spiritual questions, must be 'evidence-based' and this must include the search for answers to spiritual questions. Pope Emeritus Benedict XVI affirmed this when he gave a talk on the 'Crisis of Culture', a crisis that is affecting the West. He referred to Christianity as the 'Religion of the Logos' because this is the Greek for 'word', 'reason', 'meaning' or 'intelligence'.

He said: "From the beginning, Christianity has understood itself as the religion of the Logos, as the religion according to reason. Today, this should be precisely Christianity's strength, in so far as the problem is whether the world comes from the irrational, and reason is no other than a 'sub-product' on occasion even harmful of its development – or whether the world comes from reason, and is, as a consequence, its criterion and goal…we Christians must be very careful to remain faithful to this fundamental line: to live a faith that comes from the Logos, from creative reason, and that, because of this, is also open to all that is truly rational."

The question then arises as to what admissible evidence in this search for truth is. Faith is not a blind leap in the dark but a commitment based on evidence. We wait for a train because there is evidence in the timetable that a train will come approximately at the time prophesied. It is a tragedy that some of those who deny the possibility of there being a creator limit themselves in what evidence they will accept. When Nikita Khrushchev was leader of the Soviet bloc, he gave a speech at the plenum of the Central Committee of the Communist Party of the Soviet Union about the state's anti-religious campaign. He gave as evidence the experience of the first Soviet cosmonaut, Yuri Gagarin, saying,

"Gagarin flew into space but didn't see any god there."

Clearly such an argument limits the search for God to sight. The obvious response would be to broaden the parameters and say,

"If he had opened the door, he could have done."

Incidentally Yuri Gagarin was a member of the Russian Orthodox Church. This story illustrates how easy it is for evidence to be twisted or misused by someone to further their particular goal.

Up till now, it has only been the Christians who have been required to show evidence for their beliefs. When will the atheists be asked to show the evidence for their beliefs? They make many assumptions that cannot stand without there being a creator. Which belief system, secularism or a creator, most adequately accounts for what we see and hold dear in this world?

Chapter 2
Is There a God?

A popular writer, Yuval Noah Harari has suggested that science can explain nearly everything. One of his books is called *Homo Deus*, Latin for *Man is God*. He thinks that with all the advances that man has made in the sciences, our destiny rests in our own hands alone. He suggests that to reach 'nirvana' or the perfect life, mankind must firstly abolish death and then upgrade humans so that they will be gods. But can such a goal be achieved? At the end of his book *Sapiens, a brief history of mankind,* he wrote, "Today, it (homo sapiens) stands on the verge of becoming a god, poised to acquire not only eternal youth, but also the divine abilities of creation and destruction."[4]

He does however go on to recognise that there is a major problem with this idea – people.

"Worst still, humans seem to be more irresponsible than ever. Self-made gods with only the laws of physics to keep us company, we are accountable to no one. Is there anything more dangerous than dissatisfied and irresponsible gods who don't know what they want."[5]

Harari is very critical of those who build up structures based on false stories. He illustrates this point by criticising the Roman Catholic church:

" According to this story, if a Catholic priest dressed in his sacred garments solemnly, said the right words at the right moment, mundane bread and wine turned into God's flesh and blood. The priest exclaimed, *Hoc est corpus meum*

---

[4] Yuval Noah Harari, 'Sapiens, a brief history of humankind', Vintage, Penguin, 2011 p. 465

[5] Yuval Noah Harari, 'Sapiens, a brief history of humankind', Vintage, Penguin, 2011 p. 466

(Latin for 'This is my body') and hocus pocus – the bread turned into Christ's flesh."[6]

It is so easy to create 'straw men' and then knock them down. The real question is much bigger than the doctrines of the Roman Catholic Mass. What really matters is whether there really is a creator to whom we are all responsible and how we can find answers about how we should live.

Advanced Man and the Relevance of God

There have been many great technological advances. We can fly in aeroplanes, bionic limbs can be made, brain implants enable people to hear and possibly to see. We can use nuclear power and see the inside of bodies with scanners. The question is whether such advances can make God irrelevant. This has always been man's problem – we want to be supreme over everything. At the beginning of the Bible, Adam and Eve faced this very temptation: "And the Lord God commanded the man, "You are free to eat from any tree in the garden but you must not eat of the tree of the knowledge of good and evil, for when you eat of it you will surely die."" Genesis 2:16–17

Man is free to make many decisions, the only area we are forbidden to indulge in is to redefine what is right and wrong, that God says is his prerogative and his alone. There are many ways we can react to this. We may say, I want to be the arbiter of what I can and cannot do and I reject authority. Adam and Eve made that decision, just as we have made the decision to follow their example.

Religious Political Control

A religious authority, such as Islamic Sharia law, Jewish Rabbinical law or atheistic communism may assume control of a society but this nearly always ends eventually with disastrous consequences. Sudan suffered from thirty years of Sharia law after the Islamic revolution and the Islamic government of the despotic President Omar al-Bashir. In 1991, a Muslim clan chief, Abdulla Yousef, had a vision and he and his entire clan of around a hundred people became Christians. In 1994, Abdulla and several of the new Christians were

---

[6] Yuval Noah Harari, 'Sapiens, a brief history of humankind', Vintage, Penguin, 2011 p. 34

arrested and were sentenced to one hundred lashes. They were told that if they did not return to Islam they would be executed. Abdulla and a friend refused and were executed by crucifixion that August.

In April 2019, there was another military coup that ousted this government and a civilian government was installed which has given the much needed religious and social freedoms that people longed for. No longer are people executed for apostasy from Islam such as happened in the past although tensions are still ongoing.

A better option is to have rule by consensus but democracy can be abused as seen in Nazi Germany where the National Socialists eventually had the support of the majority of society but then dictatorship took over.

Clearly all societies need law, but societies work far better when the main control of its members is an internal moral code that the majority of individuals hold, and not through external regulations and punishments. When law is maintained because of authoritarian governments or religious authorities, there will always be resistance and rebellion.

The ideal option is for this moral code to be the result of a personal surrender to the rule of a beneficent loving God. Jesus antagonised the Jewish rulers of his day because he undermined their Rabbinical law which he contrasted with God's law. For example, he rejected their strict interpretation of what was permitted to be done on the sabbath. Instead, he put himself right at the centre of how God wanted all people to live. He claimed that he is God's law and living with him is the door to eternal life. Jesus said to some Pharisees, " I tell you the truth, if anyone keeps my word, he will never see death."

To this the Pharisees replied, "Are you greater than our father Abraham? He died and so did the prophets. **Who do you think you are**?" John 8:52–53

The political thinker, Edmund Burke (1729–1797) noted that society cannot exist, "…unless a controlling power upon will and appetite be placed somewhere; and the less of it there is within, the more there must be without."

Burke strongly argued that society works best when individuals have these constrains inbuilt within people. How can this be achieved?

What a great question! Anyone can find the answer to this vital question by reading through the twenty-one chapters of John's gospel where Jesus claims that he alone gives his followers both freedom and self-control.

Consequences of the Rejection of God

In the name of freedom, many have wrongly associated religious laws for God's law and have, as a consequence rejected the concept of God altogether. A major problem is that we then reject what we instinctively know to be real, we reject the hope of forgiveness, the hope of eternal life, as well as the most powerful check on our behaviour. This is nothing new, King David noticed, around 1000BC,

"**The fool has said in his heart, there is no God**. They are corrupt, their deeds are vile; there is no-one who does good." Psalm 14:1

The Hebrew word translated 'fool' means one who is morally deficient. When an individual wants to live their own way, as opposed to God's way, they usually come to the conclusion that there is no God. An earlier Psalm makes this point,

"**In his pride, the wicked does not seek him (the LORD)**; in all his thoughts there is no room for God." Psalm 10:4

"Why does the wicked man revile God?" **Why does he say to himself, "He won't call me to account**." Psalm 10:13

It used to be thought that when an ostrich sees danger, it may bury its head in the ground! This is not true. As flightless birds, ostriches are unable to build nests in trees, so they lay their eggs in holes dug in the ground. To make sure that the eggs are evenly heated, they occasionally stick their heads into the nest to rotate the eggs, which makes it look like they're trying to hide – hence the myth. An ostrich trying to hide from predators in this way wouldn't last for long.

Mankind is more like the ostrich myth than we like to admit. How few atheists and agnostics have really studied the evidence, both objective and subjective, that there must be a God. The evidence that Jesus is that God is also very strong. Jesus does fulfil the Old Testament prophecies, he certainly lived, was crucified and those around him had no doubts that he rose from the dead. What he taught resonates with the deepest desires and instincts within us.

When the writer Aldous Huxley was an old man, he was asked whether he had ever considered the Christian faith. He replied in a manner that only an older person could reply, honestly acknowledging that he had inner motives for rejecting God:

"I had motives for not wanting the world to have a meaning; consequently, assumed that it had not; and was able without any difficulty to find satisfying reasons for this assumption. The philosopher who finds no meaning for this world is not concerned exclusively with the problem of pure metaphysics; he is also concerned to prove that there is no valid reason why he personally should not do as he wants to. For myself, the philosophy of meaninglessness was essentially an instrument of liberation, sexual and political."[7]

Not only do people have emotional needs for God but we all have personal reasons why we want to reject him. If there is a God, he has the right to control how I should live. In a court of law, a judge is not permitted to become involved in any case in which he has an interest because it is inevitable that there would be some bias in his judgment. Yet there is clearly much bias in the decisions people make about the place given to God and Jesus in people's lives. As the late Timothy Keller has said, " We must be sceptical of our scepticism."

Consequences of Rejecting God

Rejecting the sovereignty of God may be a means to justify one's lifestyle but it does not mean that there is no God and that there is no judgment to come. The Bible is clear,

"Just as man is destined to die once and **after that face judgment**; so Christ was sacrificed once to take away the sins of many people." Hebrews 9:27

The essence of the Christian message is that Jesus is the embodied Son of God who created us and to whom he offers eternal life by taking responsibility for the sins of His people.

Another early story in the Bible is that of the Tower of Babel. The people of Babel thought,

"Come let us build **ourselves** a city, with a tower that **reaches to the heavens**, so that we may **make a name for ourselves** and not be scattered…**but the Lord came down to see the city…that the men were building**. So the LORD scattered them from there all over the earth." Genesis 11:5–9

This people wanted to 'reach the heavens' to be gods themselves, so it is no surprise that the one true God intervened. Ultimately he always does.

These claims of humans hoping to be gods can be contrasted with the Bible's claim that God became a human so that we humans could become children of

---

[7] Aldous Huxley, Ends and Means (New York, NY: Harper & Brothers Publishers, 1937), 270.

God. The solution to the problem of death is through repentance and commitment to Jesus Christ. Those who believe in him and are committed to living with and for him are promised that they will also be resurrected with him. Jesus himself made the following claim:

" I am the way, the truth and the life. No one comes to the Father except through me." John 14:6

When two of Jesus' apostles stood before the Sanhedrin, the ruling body who had recently arranged for the execution of Jesus, they confidently affirmed,

" Salvation is found in no-one else, for there is no other name under heaven given to men by which we must be saved." Acts 4:12

The emphasis of the whole Bible is that man's greatest problem is our natural rebellion against the rule of God. Although God is a God of love, there is a limit to how long his tolerance will last. He described his character to Moses on Mount Sinai,

" The LORD, the LORD, the compassionate and gracious God, slow to anger, abounding in love and faithfulness, maintaining love to thousands, and forgiving wickedness, rebellion and sin. Yet he does not leave the guilty unpunished." Exodus 34:6–7

The unforgivable sin is a rejection of what God says about Jesus because he alone is the key to eternal life. The Bible stresses that sin is essentially the rejection of God's sovereignty over us and it teaches that every human being will ultimately face God's judgment for what we have done with our lives. On that basis, we all face God's wrath because no one, religious or not, is naturally good enough for God. When we look to ourselves for salvation, it is as stupid as a man trying to reach heaven by pulling hard on his shoelaces! The prophet Jeremiah wrote around 600BC,

"Cursed is the one who trusts in man, who depends on flesh for his strength and whose heart turns away from the LORD." Jeremiah 17:5

Jeremiah contrasts such humanists with those whose ambition is to live with and for God.

"But blessed is the man who trusts in the LORD, whose confidence is in him. He will be like a tree planted by the water that sends out its roots by the stream. It does not fear when the heat comes; its leaves are always green. It has no worries in a year of drought and never fails to bear fruit." Jeremiah 17:7–8

Today there is much pressure on people to live apart from God, 'to do their own thing' and to find satisfaction, even if only short term, gratifying their emotional desires. God scoffs at such thinking that is increasingly universal. This is the great world war that is raging at the moment. An ancient psalmist recognised that this has always been man's problem:

"Why do the nations conspire and the people's plot in vain? The kings of the earth rise up and the ruler's **band together against the Lord and against his anointed**, saying, 'Let us break their chains and throw off their shackles'. **The One enthroned in heaven laughs the Lord scoffs at them**. He rebukes them in his anger and terrifies them in his wrath, saying, 'I have installed my king on Zion, my holy mountain'. I will proclaim the Lord's decree: He said to me, '**You are my son; today I have become your father. Ask me and I will make the nations your inheritance, the ends of the earth your possession**. You will break them with a rod of iron; you will dash them to pieces like pottery'. Therefore, you kings, be wise; be warned, you rulers of the earth. **Serve the Lord with fear and celebrate his rule with trembling. Kiss his son or he will be angry,** and your way will lead to your destruction, for his wrath can flare up in a moment. Blessed is all who take refuge in him." Psalm 2

This psalm recognises that Jehovah will have a Son, the Son of God. Ultimately all people decide who is to be God. Essentially, we will take this role to ourselves or abrogate it to one person or to others. We all worship somebody or something.

In a celebrated 2005 commencement address at Kenyon College, famed author David Foster Wallace told those gathered that atheism itself doesn't really exist:

"In the day-to-day trenches of adult life, **there is actually no such thing as atheism. There is no such thing as not worshipping. Everybody worships**. The only choice we get is what to worship. And an outstanding reason for choosing some sort of God or spiritual-type thing to worship – be it J.C. or Allah, be it Yahweh or the Wiccan mother-goddess or the Four Noble Truths or some infrangible set of ethical principles – is that pretty much anything else you worship will eat you alive. If you worship money and things – if they are where you tap real meaning in life – then you will never have enough. Never feel you have enough. It's the truth. Worship your own body and beauty and sexual allure and you will always feel ugly, and when time and age start showing, you will die a million deaths before they finally plant you. On one level, we all know this stuff already – it's been codified as myths, proverbs, clichés, bromides, epigrams, parables: the skeleton of every great story. The trick is keeping the truth up-front in daily consciousness. Worship power – you will feel weak and afraid, and you will need ever more power over others to keep the fear at bay. Worship your intellect, being seen as smart – you will end up feeling stupid, a fraud, always on the verge of being found out. And so on."

People can feel secure because they are in a religion, an organisation or even a church that promises its members security. Jesus and his apostles make it very clear that no security can be found there. People may be ardent members of a religion, may even be active in their church and passed through many of the prescribed rituals and yet not be right with God. The key question that we all need to answer is, "On what basis can someone like me ever be acceptable to a holy God?" Jesus and his apostles teach that no-one can be acceptable to God by the way they live, that salvation is a gift of God and this is only given to those who are committed to live under the authority of Jesus Christ, God's only Son.

The most important question that all should ask is, "Is this story about Jesus true?" If it is, then radical changes in lifestyles and ambitions will be needed. If it isn't, "What hope do we have?"

Chapter 3
Science

Science can only explain how a machine, system or organism works – it is about technology. It cannot explain why they are here. It is easy for the two to get muddled. Professor Stephen Hawking acknowledged this, saying,

"Although science may solve the problem of how the universe began, it cannot solve the question, 'Why does it bother to exist?'"

Yet how often people blindly say that science has supplied all the answers. It hasn't. Sir William Bragg, a Nobel Prize-winning Physicist said,

"From religion comes man's purpose, from science his power to achieve it. Some people ask if religion and science are opposed to each other. They are in the same way that the thumb and fingers are opposed to one another. It is an opposition by which anything can be grasped."

It is no coincidence that the renaissance of science was associated with the rediscovery of the significance of the Bible as God's word to man. This teaches that God made the world according to plan, with order and laws. Many of the early scientists were deeply committed Christians who were encouraged to discover these laws. These scientists include, Galileo (1654–1642), Babbage (1791–1871), Kepler (1571–1630), Mendel (1822–1884)Pascal (1623–1662), Pasteur (1822–1895), Boyle (1627–1691), Kelvin (1824–1907), Newton (1642–1727), Clerk Maxwell (1831–1879) and Faraday (1791–1867).

Believing in a rational creator God meant that there was a basis for the laws governing his creation and that these could be investigated. Thus Kepler, who defined the elliptical orbit of the planets, recognised that science was, "Thinking God's thoughts after him." It is only by beginning with God that we can make sense of science, its rationality and laws.

The universe is expanding at massive speeds away from a centre. This suggests that there was a finite beginning. The level of background radiation exactly matches the current calculations about what would be expected if there was an initial 'Big Bang'. This raises many questions. How did nothing explode in such a way as to result in a world with human beings living on it?

Our experience teaches us that everything has a cause. This is why the Big Bang theory is so unsettling to many atheists. John Maddox was the editor of the elite scientific magazine 'Nature'. He stated that the theory of the universe having a beginning was 'thoroughly unacceptable' as it suggested an 'ultimate origin of our world' and so giving those who believe in there being a creator God 'ample justification for their belief'.[8] By such statements, he has relegated science to a place behind personal interest.

A crashing sound from the kitchen is usually caused by the dropping of some crockery or glass onto the floor – there is always an explanation or cause. It is similarly most unscientific to suggest that the universe appeared without a cause.

The physical constants of the universe had to be set before the universe came into being. They control all physical, chemical and biological processes. Yet they are all set at precisely the right values for our world and the universe to exist and work.

One example is found in the precise balance between the force of gravity and the electromagnetic force. If there were a change in that ratio by just one in 10^{40} (ten with forty noughts after it), planets would either be so small or so large that life could not exist. To get all the constants right, if this is the only universe, is impossible – unless there is a divine designer. To counter this problem, it has been proposed that there might have been an infinite number of other universes – the 'multiverse theory'. There is no evidence for this whatsoever; it is sheer speculation as the alternative is unwanted. Michael Hanlon wrote in 'New Scientist',

"When physicists whisk us into the realms of 'multiverses' and universe-gobbling particles, it is time to ask whether there is something amiss."[9]

It is far more reasonable to hold that a divine creator set these constants.

---

[8] John Maddox, 'Down with the Big Bang', Nature 1989 340:425
[9] Michael Hanlon, 'Reality check Required' New Scientist 2008 Feb p. 22

Anthropic principle

There are many remarkable design features of our world and its place in the universe that enable man to live on earth. These together are called the 'Anthropic Principle', a phrase coined by Brandon Carter, a Cambridge physicist in 1973. *Anthropos* is Greek for man. For life to be possible on a planet, more than 128 criteria[10] need to be precisely right.

The Astro-physicist Neil deGrasse Tyson has stated,

"The universe is a deadly place. At every opportunity, it's trying to kill us."[11]

Anywhere else in space is deadly. Lethal or absent atmospheres, cosmic radiation, gamma ray bursts, solar and stellar flares, black holes, asteroids and the like all make life anywhere else in the universe, as far as we know thus far, impossible. Our world is a remarkable and exceptionally safe oasis. The universe has around 150 million galaxies and each of these has around 150 million stars and most stars have planets of some kind. Yet statistically it is almost certain that none of these would have the conditions necessary to support life. Indeed, the chance of ever finding a planet with all the properties of earth is virtually impossible statistically. Yet we are here!

The list of extraordinary coincidences in the fine tuning of the balancing constants of our universe, that allow life to exist, is continuing to enlarge. Details of these can be found in the book, *The Creator and the Cosmos* by Hugh Ross.[12]

For example: Protons are the positively charged subatomic particles which, along with neutrons form the nucleus of an atom (around which negatively charged electrons orbit). Protons just happen to be 1,836 times larger than electrons. If they were a little bigger or a little smaller, we would not exist (because atoms could not form the molecules life requires). So how did protons end up being 1,836 times larger than electrons? Why not 100 times larger or 100,000 times? Why not smaller? Of all the possible variables, how did protons end up being just the right size? Was it luck or planning?

The rate of the expansion of the universe, one second after the big bang, was controlled by the balance between the power of gravity and the power of the

---

[10] Hugh Ross, 'The Creator and the Cosmos', NavPress 2001 p. 194
[11] Big Think Mentor, June 27, 2013, bigthink.com/big-think-mentor/neil-degrasse-tyson-caught-on-camera-the-universe-is-trying-to-kill-you.
[12] Hugh Ross, 'The Creator and the Cosmos' NavPress 2001 p.145–157, 245–248

expansive explosion. Professor Stephen Hawking has calculated that if the rate of expansion had been smaller by just one part in a hundred thousand million then the universe would have collapsed in on itself because of the power of gravity.

It is generally assumed by scientists that impossibility is defined as anything higher than a chance of 1 in 10 raised to the power 50. Professor Davies has calculated that a change in the power of gravity by just 1 in 10 raised to the power 100 would have prevented the universe from forming. The fact that the universe has formed raises the question as to how all these constants are precisely right. Prof Davies has concluded,

"Through my scientific work I have come to believe more and more strongly that the physical universe is put together with an ingenuity so astonishing that I cannot merely accept it as a brute fact."[13]

It would appear that the earth is specifically 'made for man'. Freeman Dyson wrote in 'Scientific American',

"As we look out into the universe and identify the many accidents of physics and astronomy that have worked together for our benefit, it almost seems as if the universe must in some sense have known that we were coming."[14]

Arno Penzias, the Nobel Prize winner, who discovered the background radiation in space, summarised his understanding,

"Astronomy leads us to a unique event, a universe which was created out of nothing, one with the very delicate balance needed to provide exactly the right conditions required to permit life, and one which has an underlying (one might say 'supernatural') plan."

Sir Isaac Newton, the great seventeenth century scientist who gave us our understanding of gravity, built a model of the solar system to help him with his work. A fellow scientist, who was an atheist, came to visit him and admired the model.

"Who made this?" he asked.

"Nobody," replied Newton.

"Don't be ridiculous, someone made it."

---

[13] Paul Davies, 'The Mind of God', New York, Simon and Shuster 1992 p. 169
[14] Freeman Dyson, Scientific American, 225.25 (1971)

"If no one has a problem in realising that a model needs a maker, why is it such a problem when confronted with the real universe?" Newton poignantly responded.

Rules in nature

This world works according to rules that can often be expressed mathematically. The sun rises in the morning and goes down at night at regular times. The stars don't change positions but the planets do move in a methodical way. Beautiful rhythmic patterns can be seen in nature.

Sunflower seeds grow in an intricate pattern of interwoven spirals that go in both clockwise and anti-clockwise directions and are at different angles. The number of spirals tend to be either 21 and 34, 34 and 55, 55 and 89, or 89 and 144. The same relationship can be seen when counting the spirals on fir cones. These have either 8 spirals from one side and 13 from the other, or 5 spirals from one side and 8 from the other. The number of diagonals on a pineapple are often 8 in one direction and 13 in the other. These numbers just happen to be in the Fibonacci sequence, in which each number is the sum of the two preceding ones. This sequence is therefore, 0, 1, 1, 2, 3, 5, 8, 13, 21, 34, 55, 89, 144.

The fact that the universe and everything in it works according to mathematical principles is astounding. Science cannot explain this; yet it is a repeated observation and from this comes the assumption that the world will continue to work according to these rules. Paul Davies has commented,

"Just because the sun has risen every day of your life, there is no guarantee that it will rise tomorrow. The belief that it will – that there are indeed dependable regularities of nature – is an act of faith, but one which is indispensable to the progress of science."[15]

Professor John Polkinghorne said,

"Science does not explain the mathematical intelligibility of the physical world, for it is part of science's founding faith that it is so."[16]

Eugene Wigner, a Nobel Laureate in Physics, made a similar comment,

---

[15] Paul Davies, "The Mind of God," London, Simon and Schuster, 1992 p. 81
[16] John Polkinghorne, "Reason and Reality," SPCK, 1991 p.76

"The enormous usefulness of mathematics in the natural sciences is something bordering on the mysterious, and there is no rational explanation…it is an article of faith."[17]

This is important for two reasons. Firstly, all knowledge is clearly built on 'faith assumptions' – faith is not just a religious phenomenon. Secondly there is the conundrum as to how this has happened. Mathematical truths seem to have been present before the universe began as everything is based on them.

The Bible explains this. The God who created the universe is a rational God. He does not design randomly but works according to principles. He also constantly uses reason to remind people of the evidence that he exists and therefore why they should follow his ways. The Biblical God is also a very gracious God who appreciates beauty, honour and repentance. However, he has personality and does get angry when nations and individuals leave him out of their thinking and go their own selfish and immoral ways. This is a remarkable combination when he is contrasted with other gods.

The Oxford Professor, Richard Swinburne, is very clear that to point out aspects of obvious design in the universe is not to fall into the 'God of the Gaps' trap, where anything difficult to understand is explained as the intervention of God. He wrote,

"I am not postulating a 'God of the gaps', a God merely to explain the things that science has not yet explained. I am postulating a God to explain why science explains; I do not deny that science explains, but I postulate God to explain why science explains."

There must be a God for there to be a rational world which works according to rules. Someone set these rules. They are so set as not just to be functional but aesthetic as well.

Examples such as this could be repeated again and again. It would be as absurd to suggest that 'The Mona Lisa' picture in the Louvre came about by chance and that there was no Leonardo da Vinci or other artist who painted it. It is just as silly to say that there is no design or designer in the universe. The chance of the universe developing without a designer is so minute as to be impossible. There must have been a mind that designed and controlled all that has happened.

---

[17] E.P. Wigner, "The Unreasonable Effectiveness of Mathematics," Communications in Pure and Applied Mathematics, 13 (1960) pp. 1–14

Sir Fred Hoyle, the astrophysicist, was not a Christian but he concluded, "I do not believe that any scientist who examined the evidence would fail to draw the inference that the laws of nuclear physics have been deliberately designed with regard to the consequences they produce within the stars."[18]

"A commonsense interpretation of the facts suggests that a super intellect has monkeyed with physics, as well as with chemistry and biology and that there are no blind forces worth speaking about in nature."[19]

Professor Owen Gingerich, an astronomer at Harvard University agreed,

"Fred Hoyle and I differ on lots of questions, but on this we agree: a common sense and satisfying interpretation of our world suggests the designing hand of a super intelligence."

Professor Paul Davies moved from promoting atheism in 1983 to conceding in 1984, "The laws (of physics) …seem themselves to be the product of exceedingly ingenious design."[20]

In his book *The Cosmic Blueprint*, published in 1988, Professor Davies said,

"There is for me powerful evidence that there is something going on behind it all. It seems as though somebody has fine-tuned nature's numbers to make the universe. The impression of design is overwhelming."[21]

Robin Collins, who has doctorates in both physics and philosophy has said,

"The extraordinary fine tuning of the laws and constants of nature, their beauty, their discoverability, their intelligibility – all of this combines to make the God hypothesis the most reasonable choice we have. All other theories fall short."[22]

---

[18] Fred Hoyle, "The Universe: Past and Present Reflections." Annual Review of Astronomy and Astrophysics 20 (1982)

[19] Fred Hoyle 'The Universe; past and present reflections', Annual Reviews of Astronomy and Astrophysics 1982, 20:16

[20] Paul Davies, 'Superforce', New York, Simon and Schuster, 1984 p 243

[21] Paul Davies, "The Cosmic Blueprint," New York, Simon and Schuster, 1988 p203

[22] Lee Strobel, 'The Case for a Creator: A Journalist Investigates Scientific Evidence That Points Toward God', Zondervan, 2004

The source of new genetic information

The theory of Neo-Darwinism depends upon there being many beneficial mutations that work coherently together. Yet nearly all the mutations seen in the animal kingdom are detrimental. David Demick wrote in an article on mutations,

"With thousands of examples of harmful mutations readily available, surely it would be possible to describe some positive mutations if macro-evolution is true. These would be needed not only for evolution to greater complexity but also to offset the downward pull of the many harmful mutations. But when it comes to identifying positive mutations, evolutionary scientists are strangely silent."[23]

It is very hard to conceive how major changes in organisms could be brought about by random mutations. Mutations are largely harmful effects that clearly get weeded out with time. This is why the fossil record confirms that species do not alter whilst they exist. That is why the fruit fly, which can readily develop mutations with irradiation, with sometimes bizarre effects, has not changed significantly according to the fossil records since they first appeared. The geneticist Gordon Taylor wrote,

"It is a striking but not much mentioned fact, that though geneticists have been breeding fruit flies for sixty years or more in labs all round the world, flies which produce a new generation every eleven days – they have never yet seen the emergence of a new species or even a new enzyme."[24]

The oldest insect fossils are about 400 million years old. Around 300 million years ago there suddenly appeared a wide range of insects such as cockroaches. The striking feature is that the oldest dragonflies, centipedes and flies have not changed at all over all this time. The adaptation in design needed for a fly to flap its wings 500 times a second is marked. We are totally in the dark about how insects developed.

Pierre-Paul Grassé, a former President of the French Academy of Science, acknowledges that mutations which are like 'making mistakes in the letters when copying a written text' cannot give rise to new information. This point is so important. He writes,

---

[23] David Demick, "The Blind Gunman," Impact 308 1999
[24] Gordon Rattray Taylor, "The Great Evolution Mystery," Abacus, Sphere Books, London 1984 p.48

"Mutations, in time, occur incoherently. They are not complementary to one another, nor are they cumulative in successive generations toward a given direction. They modify what pre-exists, but they do so in disorder, no matter how. As soon as some disorder, even slight, appears in an organised being, sickness, then death follow. There is no possible compromise between the phenomenon of life and anarchy."[25]

In fact, mutants usually die or are sterile. Experiments over many years have resulted in just what would be expected. Mutations do not produce beneficial, meaningful genetic code.

It is highly unlikely that a significant genetic mutation, even if beneficial, could survive without a male and female both having the same mutations and they would need to breed together if the effect was to remain. Furthermore this line must then inbreed. So two similar groups of mutants must appear at the same time, in the same place and have a particular survival advantage in that habitat. All this makes the whole thesis very farfetched indeed.

When the genetic differences between the higher apes and humans are looked at, it is seen that there are bigger differences between the gorilla and the chimp genomes than there are between the chimp and humans. There is overall a 98% similarity between the genetic makeup of chimps compared that of humans. In some segments, there are very few differences whereas in other segments there are marked differences. There are not uniform slight differences that would be expected if random mutation was the cause of the differences. This is more in keeping with the theory that a creator altered a working genetic template to produce the genome of man.

Professor Lahn, an Assistant Professor at the University of Chicago, and his team have been studying genetic differences between humans and other mammals. They examined the DNA of 214 genes involved in the foetal brain development of humans, macaque monkeys, rats and mice. They found that there were marked differences in a large number of genes and concluded that these changes must have appeared over a very short time. They concluded that a simple

---

[25] Pierre-Paul Grassé, "Evolution of Living Organisms," Academic Press New York 1977 p. 97–98

explanation involving random mutations and selection of the fittest was highly unlikely.[26]

In 1967, there was a rather tense meeting between some mathematicians and leading Darwinists at the Wistar Institute in Philadelphia. The mathematicians argued that there was nothing like enough time for the necessary multitude of small beneficial mutations to have occurred in. Thus, it was said that for an eye to develop and become even partially functional would necessitate there being huge numbers of specific mutations that would give no function until they were all present. In a report of the conference, it was said,

"There is a considerable gap in the neo-Darwinian theory of evolution, and we believe this gap to be of such a nature that it cannot be bridged with the current conception of biology."[27]

In an interview, the modern apostle of atheism, Richard Dawkins, was asked the question, "Can you give an example of a genetic mutation or an evolutionary process which can be seen to increase the information in the genome?"

He was stumped. He sat in silence in front of the camera for a full twenty seconds before asking for it to be turned off. When the filming restarted, he answered a completely different question. This short interview is available on the web and is worth seeing.[28] Whether it is a hoax I do not know but it does illustrate that there is no satisfactory scientific answer to explain the origin of new meaningful genetic code.

Fossils

The fossil record does not fit with current Darwinian theories that propose that change has been brought about by the gradual accumulation of mutations. Many years ago George Gaylord Simpson, an evolutionary palaeontologist at the

---

[26] Steve Dorus, Eric J. Vallender, Patrick D. Evans, Jeffrey R. Anderson, Sandra L. Gilbert, Michael Mahowald, Gerald J. Wyckoff, Christine M. Malcom and Bruce T. Lahn, "Accelerated Evolution of Nervous System Genes in the Origin of Homo sapiens" Cell, Volume 119, Issue 7, 29 December 2004, Pp 1027–1040

[27] Schutzenberger, M.P. (1967) "Algorithms and the Neo-Darwimian Theory of Evolution," in Mathematical Challenges to the Neo-Darwinian Interpretation of Evolution, ed P.S. Moorhead and M.M. Kaplan, Wistar Institute Press, Philadelphia, p75 Denton, Evolution: A Theory in Crisis, 1985, Adler & Adler, Publishers, Inc. pages 289

[28] https://www.youtube.com/watch?v=K0F1RtT9dZ8

American Museum of Natural History, acknowledged the absence of intermediate fossil forms throughout the plant and animal kingdoms.

Niles Eldridge, of the American Museum of Natural History reviewed the evidence for classical Darwinism and concluded that the expected evidence for changes in species was simply not there.

"I found that out back in the 1960s as I tried in vain to document examples of the kind of slow, steady directional change we all thought ought to be there, ever since Darwin told us that natural selection should leave precisely such a tell-tale signal as we collect our fossils up cliff faces. I found instead that once species appear in the fossil record, they tend not to change much at all. Species remain imperturbably, implacably resistant to change as a matter of course."[29]

In 1970, two American palaeontologists, Stephen Jay Gould of Harvard University and Niles Eldridge of the American Museum of Natural History, had recognised that stasis of species was the norm and they published an alternative theory called 'punctuated equilibrium'. Essentially they proposed that evolution must have occurred through sudden dramatic genetic mutations in order to account for the sudden appearances of new species in fossil records. Although this theory fitted the evidence better, it floundered because no reasonable mechanism could be thought of by which this could have occurred.

A large number of mutations would be necessary and these must all be to a plan. That would necessitate a designer. Random major genetic changes cause either death or monstrosities. And such a creature would have to find another genetically similar mate to continue the line. Ernest Mayr a Darwinist, has commented on the possibility of major sudden random mutations causing new species,

"To believe that such a drastic mutation would produce a viable new type, capable of occupying a new adaptive zone, is equivalent to believing in miracles. The finding of a suitable mate for the 'hopeless monster' and the establishment of reproductive isolation from the normal members of the parental population seem to me insurmountable difficulties."[30]

It is as if a dinosaur laid an egg and out came a bird. A similar major change would have to occur in another egg in the same geographical area and at the same

---

[29] Niles Eldridge, "Reinventing Darwin" 1995, p77

[30] Ernest Mayr, "Populations, species and Evolution" Cambridge, Mass. Belknap Press, 1970, p. 235

time, yet of the opposite sex for the new line to propagate. For this to have all occurred randomly is not a viable proposition.

Irreducible complexity

Michael Behe wrote a book called *Darwin's Black Box* in which he highlighted this problem. He gives the example of the retina cell, which cannot transform a photon of light into an impulse along the optic nerve unless it has at least two hundred enzymes all in the right sequence and all fully working. There is no benefit and no 'survival of the fittest' unless everything is in place. How could that happen randomly? He also discusses the chemical motor at the base of the flagellum of a bacterium. This motor can turn the flagellum up to ten thousand revolutions a minute in either direction. It is made up of many proteins, all in the right place. Such complex mechanisms cannot work unless everything is in place to start with. They cannot have gradually developed as there was no survival advantage until the whole works.

Christian de Duve wrote in *A Guided Tour of the Living Cell* (Nobel laureate and organic chemist)

"If you equate the probability of the birth of a bacteria cell to chance assembly of its atoms, eternity will not suffice to produce one. Faced with the enormous sum of lucky draws behind the success of the evolutionary game, one may legitimately wonder to what extent this success is actually written into the fabric of the universe."

Simon Conway Morris, the eminent paleontologist who discovered the significance of the Cambrian explosion of animal life, wrote in his seminal book *Life's Solutions* that he is 'convinced' that nature's success in the lottery of life has 'metaphysical implications.'

DNA

The existence of this remarkable nucleic acid is surely an astounding miracle. How could it have developed randomly without there being a designer. Professor Anthony Flew, Professor of Philosophy, former atheist, author, and debater said,

"It is, for example, impossible for evolution to account for the fact than one single cell can carry more data than all the volumes of the Encyclopedia Britannica put together."

"It now seems to me that the findings of more than fifty years of DNA research have provided materials for a new and enormously powerful argument to design."

He changed his mind and came to the conclusion that there had to be a mind, a God, behind the creation of the DNA system.

Designed?

John's record of the story of Jesus begins with the words,

"In the beginning was the word (Greek 'logos') and the word was with God and the word was God." John 1:1

This word 'logos' could be translated 'information' or even 'code'. The God of the Bible clearly teaches that it was God who designed this world and who is involved in every detail of life and its continuation throughout the generations. The God of the Bible is a creator who also has both personality and values. A preacher put it this way,

"The existence of the world points to a cause, the order of the universe suggests a mind, the beauty of nature a soul, the bountifulness of life a heart."[31]

The concept of a supernatural God who is outside his created universe and somehow controls all that goes on is strange to modern man. We have seldom experienced the supernatural or the miraculous and doubt its existence. Yet here in the world of cosmology and biology we have the miraculous staring at us in the face. God has clearly intervened. The concept of a creator immediately gives rise to the charge of invoking a 'God of the Gaps' where anything we cannot understand is attributed to God. Advances in science would have been greatly restricted if difficult problems were simply attributed to God's direct intervention. However, there must, at some stage in the world's creation, be a time when God did intervene. Clearly, he must have set the constants of physics when the world began. Clearly, he has been involved in creation. How and how often he has intervened supernaturally can be debated but life cannot be an accident. Miracles almost by definition are rare, but if God can raise Jesus from the dead and give prophetic details about his coming in the old Jewish Scriptures then he is able to intervene at any stage in his creation to cause what we see today. Many parents think that the creation of a baby is miraculous.

---

[31] Walter F Adeney (1849–1920) in Great Sermons ed Warren Wiersbe (1993) p4

The majesty of this creation is also clear for any who have eyes to see it. Agur, the writer of the penultimate chapter of the Book of Proverbs had this to say, "Who has established all the ends of the earth? What is his name and the name of his son? Tell me if you know." Proverbs 30:4

I have written in more detail on the relationship between science and God in my book, *Science and God, Enemies or Allies*. Helpful information on the scientific evidence for a creator can also to be found in the books written by Hugh Ross and the other scholars of the 'Reasons to Believe' organization.

Chapter 4
What If There Is No God?

When I was a student, Francis Schaeffer, the great Christian philosopher, used to visit Cambridge University regularly to teach a group of students. One of the concepts I remember him teaching was that, when talking to people with a different world view, such as atheists, agnostics, existentialists or whatever, he would spend much time talking with them to show the negative, illogical and often disastrous consequences of that way of thinking. Only then would he go on to explain the reasons why he had become a Christian.

The Consequences of There Being No God

If mankind accidentally evolved from slime in a godless world, there can be no 'real' values, all must be make-believe and therefore optional. If there is no personal God who created us, such traits have to be downgraded to interesting side effects of our evolution. Clearly, they can have no 'otherworldly' significance, if life is an accident. These values would not be worth dying for. If however, we were created 'in God's image', then God's values would be part of our make-up. It is no coincidence that the values people most admire are characteristics of Jesus Christ.

Some modern thinkers have recognised the importance of these values but want to try and give them substance without invoking a creator. They have been described as 'ultimate realities' although logically there can be nothing ultimate about them without there being an ultimate God, as Plato clearly understood. G. K. Chesterton astutely put it this way,

"God is not a symbol of Goodness: Goodness is a symbol of God."

The instincts that recognise these essential values are common to all people. Goodness is recognised by our consciences, beauty in our imaginations and truth in our rational minds. Goodness is cherished when seen in others. A beautiful scene whispers to us that there is a transcendent aspect to our lives; it is a reflection of 'another world'. George Steiner thought beauty was 'an echo of the presence of other.'

We live in a society that increasingly thinks 'God is dead'. Some still accept God in theory but in practice he is largely irrelevant to them – they live as practical atheists. The strange thing is that many who think like this still consider life should be lived on Christian principles – at least by others.

One hundred years ago the philosopher Friedrich Nietzsche foretold that within a century God would 'be dead' in society. He rightly scorned those who acknowledged this in their thinking but kept the old morality and duties. George Eliot, the author who wrote 'Middlemarch' and 'Mill on the Floss' was such a person. She wrote,

"God is inconceivable and immortality unbelievable but duty is nevertheless peremptory and absolute."

When Alexander Solzhenitsyn gave his Templeton Prize address, he said that the tragedy of the modern world was, "You have forgotten God." In a subsequent interview with Bernard Levin, published in the Times, he explained that he now considered that the goal of man is 'not happiness but spiritual growth'. He had learned this from Jesus.

Solomon understood that this is man's greatest problem. Near the beginning of the book of Proverbs he said, "The fear of the LORD is the beginning of knowledge. " Proverbs 1:7

A little later he explains that everyone has made a decision on this matter,

"Since they hated knowledge and **did not choose to fear the LORD.**" Proverbs 1:29

The widespread dissatisfaction is a common symptom that comes from this refusal to allow God to hold his proper place in our lives.

No truth

This Is My Truth Tell Me Yours was the fifth studio album, released 1998 by Welsh alternative rock band *Manic Street Preachers*. In spite of this idea that people can have their own truths, there is a universal conviction that there is an ultimate reality called truth. Society is dependent on this being so. In the law courts, witnesses are giving their impressions of what really happened – what they understand to be the truth. In medicine, we use a wide variety of tests to make a right diagnosis as to what pathology is causing a patient's illness. We recognise that there is a true answer even though we may have difficulties coming to the right answer. Trust in relationships depends on people being truthful. Society is dependent on there being a real value called 'truth'.

What is truth? I discussed this with a group of medical consultants and they concluded, "Truth must be consensus." This cannot be right as consensual support for an idea can be obtained using a variety of means. Politicians with power have often tried to rewrite history when the truth is not helpful to their political aspirations. Hitler had the consensus of Germany supporting his regime yet now most Germans strongly repudiate many of his repugnant views. The majority of people used to accept Aristotle's teaching that the 'heavenly bodies' were made of an unearthly very light 'fifth substance' or, in Greek, the 'quintessence'. The consensus at one time was that the earth was the centre of the universe. The consensus was clearly wrong in the light of subsequent research.

The only definition of truth that can stand is one that relates to an absolute, as Plato recognised. Truth may thus be defined as 'a concept compatible with God'. If there is no God, there is no truth, only consensus. Some have argued that truth can only be found in physical reality but such a materialistic definition denies the value of many areas of life on which our society depends. These would include love, integrity, honour, courage and kindness. Although these values cannot be proved, our instincts affirm that they are real and important.

Without there being an absolute God, there can be no absolute truth. Everything becomes relative. Your truth may then be different to mine. Yet in science we are searching for real laws, real explanations that explain our existence. We believe in such truth. In the legal world, though witnesses may give different accounts of what happened, it is widely accepted that there is somewhere a truth of what really happened.

If our existence is a random event, then there can be no assurance that our instincts concerning truth are valid, yet we cannot live without the concept of truth.

No basis for logic

Logic also becomes unreliable. Professor Haldane astutely said,

"If my mental processes are determined wholly by the motion of atoms in my brain, I have no reason to suppose that my beliefs are true...and hence I have no reason for supposing my brain to be composed of atoms."[32]

Charles Darwin himself was concerned about this and, when elderly, wrote, "The horrid doubt always arises whether the convictions of man's mind, which has developed from the mind of lower animals, are of any value or at all trustworthy. Would anyone trust the convictions of a monkey's mind, if there are any convictions in such a mind?"[33]

All science depends upon the obvious finding that we live in a rational universe with the so-called laws of nature. How did this happen? The Bible teaches that it is the obvious evidence of design in the universe that means there must be a designer. It is our rejection of him that angers God.

"The wrath of God is being revealed from heaven against all the godlessness and wickedness of men who suppress the truth by their wickedness, since what may be known about God is plain to them, because God has made it plain to them. For since the creation of the world God's invisible qualities – his eternal power and divine nature – have been clearly seen, being understood from what has been made, so men are without excuse." Romans 1:18–20

Einstein recognised that the basis of the scientific method was the fact that the universe is rational. He astutely said, "The most incomprehensible thing about the universe is that it is comprehensible."[34]

It is this rationality that has led many philosophers to recognise that the universe must be the product of a very intelligent God. He must have a rational mathematical mind.

Science is the search for truth. If truth is defined in Plato's terms as concepts compatible with God, it is clearly nonsense to try to use science, which is a search for truth, to destroy a belief in God. God is the only basis for truth's validity.

It is remarkable how often atheists and agnostics try to argue logically that God does not exist or cannot be known. They are using the very logic that can

---

[32] J.B.S. Hldane, 'Possible Worlds' 1927, 'When I am dead'
[33] https://www.darwinproject.ac.uk/letter/DCP-LETT-13230.xml
[34] Albert Einstein, 'Letters to Solovine', New York, Philosophical Library, 1987 p.131

only be validated if there is a logical God who has created us in his image. It is rather like the speaker at Hyde Park corner who shouted out in an impassioned way,

"I am telling you the truth!" and then he got to his main point, "There is no God and there is no truth."

No morals

Without God, anything goes and the strong will determine even the morality of society. It is only because there is a supreme being who will judge us all that the atrocities of Hitler, Stalin, Pol Pot and the genocides in Ukraine, Ruanda, Sudan and Bosnia are wrong.

Nietzsche derided people as 'odious windbags of progressive optimism, who think it is possible to have Christian morality without Christian faith.' In *Twilight of the Idols* he wrote,

"They are rid of the Christian God, and now believe all the more firmly that they must cling to Christian morality…when one gives up the Christian faith, one pulls the right to Christian morality from under one's feet."[35]

This point was brilliantly put in a debate where an analogy between our reliance on God and air was made – both are invisible but are essential for life.

"Imagine a person who comes in here tonight and argues, 'no air exists' but continues to breathe air while he argues. Now intellectually, atheists continue to breathe – they continue to use reason and draw scientific conclusions (which assumes an orderly universe), to make moral judgments (which assumes absolute values) – but the atheistic view of things would in theory make such 'breathing' impossible. They are breathing God's air all the time they are arguing against him."[36]

This pressure to leave God out of our thinking is very dangerous for our or any society. Dostoevsky wrote in *The Brothers Karamozov*,

"Is there no God? Then everything is permitted."

The atheist, Richard Dawkins, has said,

---

[35] https://genius.com/Friedrich-nietzsche-twilight-of-the-idols-chap-8-annotated
[36] Greg Bahnsen, 'Prepositional Apologetics Stated and Defended', American Vision, 2010

"...a universe with a creative superintendent would be a very different kind of universe from one without.[37]"

Standards of behaviour and personal integrity will inevitably diminish, both in individuals and in society as fewer individuals do what is right before God, refusing to believe that God will ultimately be their judge. Winston Churchill reminded us that a nation cannot expect its citizens to follow Christian ethics if it fails to teach them Christian dogma.

It is perhaps significant that few recognise the opposite of integrity. It is dis-integrity or disintegration. When an individual loses the determination to do what is right before God, first his personal life, then his family life, then his societies' life and ultimately his nations' life will tend to disintegrate. This is what Gibbon thought was the cause of the 'Decline and Fall of the Roman Empire' and isn't it what we are beginning to see in this country?

The novelist William Golding, who wrote *Lord of the Flies* said,

"If God is dead, if man is the highest, good and evil are decided by majority vote."[38]

Adolf Hitler appreciated this, as he held the majority vote.

Hitler developed some of Darwin's theories into his social ideas. Darwin did try to dissociate himself from these extreme views that held that it was acceptable to exterminate the weaker people in society in order to strengthen the genetic pool and so make society stronger. Darwin thought racial groups such as aborigines and Negroes were intermediaries between apes and fully developed humans that were both intellectually and morally weaker than Europeans. He wrote in *The Descent of Man*,

"If we do not prevent...the inferior members of our society from increasing at a quicker pace than the better class of men, the nation will retrograde. "

He did think that human beings should control their own evolution,

"All do good service who aid towards this end..."[39]

It was Ernst Haeckel, a Professor of Zoology in Germany and an ardent disciple of Darwin, who popularised the logical consequences of Darwinism. He wrote, "What good does it do to humanity to maintain artificially and rear the

---

[37] Richard Dawkins, 'The God Delusion' Bantam Press, 2006 p. 55

[38] http://inplainsite.org/html/god_in_a_postmodern_world.html

[39] Charles Darwin, 'The Descent of Man', 1871, Penguin Books quoted by Sheena Tyler, 'Origins 41' Sept 2005 p16

thousands of cripples, deaf mutes, idiots, etc who are born every year with an hereditary burden of incurable disease?"[40]

He encouraged 'involuntary euthanasia', the active killing of 'the hundreds of thousands of incurables – lunatics, lepers, people with cancer, etc.' Haeckel also recommended the 'indiscriminate destruction of all incorrigible criminals.'

Haeckel's views became very popular in Germany. They were accepted by Hitler and became the basis for the extermination of the Jews, the insane, gypsies and other undesirables such as unwanted children, by the third Reich regime. It is important to remember that many of these killings were undertaken by ordinary doctors and nurses who were following approved protocols.[41]

Jeremy Rifkin believes in the 'New Age' philosophy. Towards the end of his book *Algeny*, he discusses the effect that Darwinism logically brings with it.

"This is evolution. We no longer feel ourselves to be guests in someone else's home and therefore obliged to make our behaviour conform to a set of pre-existing cosmic rules. It is our creation now. We make the rules. We establish the parameters of reality. We create the world and because we do we no longer have to justify our behaviour. We are now the architects of the universe. We are responsible, nothing outside ourselves. We are the kingdom, the power and the glory for ever and ever."[42]

The Russian novelist Fyodor Dostoevsky often wrote about the dangerous situation that ensues when men refuse to acknowledge their creator and instead make themselves gods.

When my wife and I visited the Nazi extermination camps of Auschwitz and Birkenau the truth of what happens when men become gods becomes grossly apparent. Hitler had envisaged a generation that had rejected the old ideals and boasted,

"I freed Germany from the stupid and degrading fallacies of conscience and morality. We will train young people before whom the world will tremble. I want young people capable of violence – imperious, relentless and cruel."[43]

---

[40] Ernst Haeckel, 'The Wonders of Life, 1904

[41] Ernest Haeckel, 'The History of Creation', translated by E.R Lancaster, Appleton, New York, 1901, quoted by Sheena Tyler, 'Origins 41' Sept 2005 p18

[42] Jeremy Rifkin, 'Algeny', Viking Press, 1983

[43] https://ejewishphilanthropy.com/what-would-moses-say-of-nietzsche-hitler-and-the-freedom-to-hurt-others-shavuot-5780/

When man turns his back on God, morality becomes arbitrary. The agenda can be set by the man who is most powerful.

Totalitarianism increases

So when integrity diminishes, external state control or totalitarianism increases with all its associated problems. Kafka's book *The Castle* describes a world with problems similar to those we are beginning to see today. It describes a world where there is overwhelming bureaucratic power and authority. The telephone exchanges produce more muddles than connections. Bureaucracy drowns human beings in a deluge of files and forms. A stifling hierarchy makes it impossible to get through to any senior responsible people. Kafka says,

"The conveyor belt of life carries you on, no one knows where. One is more of an object, a thing, than a living creature."

The use of the word 'creature' is significant. A 'creature' has been formed by a 'creator'. In a godless world, bullying and intimidation inevitably increase. No opposition to the dictator's wishes can be permitted as the 'best' and even 'truth' is now defined by what benefits the regime.

Joseph Stalin had, in his youth, been a theological student, preparing to become a priest. However, his ambitions, mixed with Nietzsche's teaching, caused him to reject any belief in God. He pursued, with great ardour, the goal of atheistic communism instead. The name Stalin was not his real name – it means 'steel'. It was given to him by his fellow communists to reflect his steel-like determination to reach his goal. It was this characteristic that led Lenin to appoint him to lead the Communist party. His daughter, Svetlana, was present when he was dying and said he was troubled by awful hallucinations. Suddenly he sat up in bed, defiantly threw a clenched fist into the air as a defiant gesture against God and died.

No meaning

Many modern writers, such as Chekov, Kafka, Sartre and Camus reveal, "The persistent need for meaning and the gnawing sense of its elusiveness."[44]

---

[44] Terry Eagleton, 'The Meaning of Life: A Very Short Introduction', Oxford University Press, 2003 p. 58

The existentialist writer, Jean-Paul Sartre, wrote a book called *No Exit*, saying that he can see no exit from the human dilemma. If there are no real answers, make up your own and live them to the full. His philosophy emptied life of real meaning. However instinctively four fifths of people feel that their life does have meaning.[45]

A French perfume manufacturer sold its fragrances to the English with the catch phrase,

'Life is to be played by your own script.'

This reflects other current phrases such as,

'Just do it.'

'Just be.'

'Follow your dream.'

Yet Sartre's logic and conclusions are right only if you start with his atheistic presumptions.

No answer to guilt

"A guilty conscience never feels secure," said the Roman, Publius Syrus.

"Guilt is the source of sorrow, 'tis the fiend, th'avenging fiend, that follows us behind with whips and stings," said the playwright Nicholas Rowe (1674–1718).

"Suspicion always haunts the guilty mind," said William Shakespeare.

"From the body of one guilty deed, a thousand ghostly fears and haunting thoughts proceed," said William Wordsworth.

Such opinions could be multiplied many times. There is no doubt that guilt is a very destructive force in individuals. It has a 'compound interest' effect. The more sinful and guilty a person feels, the less chance there is that he will be a happy, healthy and satisfied citizen.

Yet is this sense of guilt bad for us and society? It is easy to complain when you pick up a hot cooking utensil mistakenly. Yet that feeling of pain is definitely to your benefit. It took many years for doctors to understand why people suffering from leprosy found their fingers and toes disappearing. It is because the slow growing bacterium, *Mycobacteria leprae,* invades the nerves which

---

[45] Terry Eagleton, 'The Meaning of Life: A Very Short Introduction', Oxford University Press, 2003 p. 12

subsequently cease to function. Sufferers therefore have limited or no feeling in their extremities. They don't feel the heat of a boiling kettle when they pick it up. They don't feel their toes rubbing on their sandals. Ulcers develop which slowly cause degeneration. In the same way, we can become de-sensitised if we constantly ignore our consciences.

Guilt can be painful yet it is necessary both for our society and ourselves. Some have tried to explain it away as a product of our upbringing or the effect of the church, but it must be deeper than that. People who have no connections with church tend to feel more and not less guilty.

Eric Fromm wrote in his book, *The Sane Society*,

"It is indeed amazing that, in as fundamentally an irreligious culture as ours, the sense of guilt should be so widespread and deep rooted as it is."[46]

The book *Realised Religion* reviews research on the relationship between religion and health. It concludes, "Mental Health workers need to be aware of the positive potential of religious involvement." Overall 'fully eighty per cent of psychiatric research on religion and health conclude that a faith is advantageous'. Many studies in 'Life Satisfaction' show that there is a direct relationship between spiritual commitment and contentment. A number of studies conclude, 'materialistic people generally have been found to be unhappy'. This sense of well-being is accredited to the effect of individual beliefs as well as from active involvement in religious communities and activities.[47]

The amazing fact is that we all like to be tempted. There is something exciting about it. "We won't be harmed by a little thought, will we?" A vicar was trying to help a man whose marriage was on the rocks because he had had an affair.

"I don't know how it happened," the unhappy man complained.

"I do," replied the wise vicar. "You had been thinking about these things in your imagination and found them attractive. Then, when you found yourself in the same situation, it was all too easy to fall."

An American preacher put it this way, "Sinful pleasure lures us only in anticipation, dancing before us like Salome before her uncle Herod, quite irresistible in fascination, happiness seems focused on her. But on the day that deed, long held in alluring expectation, is actually done, how swift and how

---

[46] Eric Fromm, The Sane Society, Fawcett, 1977 p. 181
[47] Theodore J. Chamberlain and Christopher A. Hall, 'Realised Religion', Research on the Relationship between Religion and Health, Templeton Foundation Press.

terrible the alteration in its aspect. It passes from anticipation to committal into memory, and will never be beautiful again."

There is not one of us who can look God in the eye with our head high. We have all failed to live as we know we should have done. Does everyone have these standards? Oh, yes. Just think how we criticise others for the things they do. Everyone knows about guilt.

It was the reality about himself that finally led the agnostic C.S. Lewis to realise how much he needed Jesus Christ.

"For the first time, I examined myself with a seriously practical purpose. And there I found what appalled me. A zoo of lusts, a bedlam of ambitions, a misery of fears, a harem of fondled hatreds. My name was Legion."[48]

The reality about my guilt and my need to be forgiven for wrongdoings are powerful arguments supporting the claims of Jesus. It is only by beginning with God that life can make sense.

Marghanita Lasky, a humanist, was involved in a television debate with a Christian. She said, "What I envy most about you Christians is your forgiveness. I have no-one to forgive me."[49]

---

[48] http://countedrighteousinchrist.blogspot.com/2012/09/the-testimony-of-c-s-lewis.html
[49] John Stott in 'The Contemporary Christian'.

Chapter 5
The Validity of Values

So much for the negative logical consequences if there were no God. The truth is that people naturally hold to values and ultimately these can only come from God. We may learn this from our parents and schools but to be true values they need to reflect the character of God. The presence of these values is further evidence of the stepping stones to faith.

Love

What most people cherish more than anything else is being in a loving relationship. To be in love means we have to sacrifice our freedom and not do as we please. Love involves considering how your partner will react to any decision you make. It requires a price to be paid, a giving up of our independence but this is so worthwhile. Even God himself is subject to this cost of love.

"God so loved the world that he gave his own son..." John 3:16

In the same way, to be good at sport or in a career inevitably requires a high price of sacrificing time, commitment and saying no to other interests. Jesus paid a high price when he entered this world to die and pay for my sin. He did this because he loves us.

Similarly, to be an effective and productive Christian will demand of us that a price is paid by us, we have to learn to say no to ourselves if we are to live for our Saviour. Repentance is costly. Yet it is by this mutual service that a loving relationship with Jesus grows. A Christian is yoked to Jesus, we are restrained but he takes the pressure because he loves us. Jesus said,

"Come to me, all you who are weary and burdened, and I will give you rest. Take my yoke upon you and learn from me for I am gentle and humble in heart and you will find rest for your souls. For my yoke is easy and my burden is light." Matthew 11:28–29

It is significant that in Hebrew the word often translated 'worship' can also mean the 'service' of someone. Love requires us to serve or worship someone.

Huang was only 22 years old, yet he was in a Chinese prison awaiting execution for murder, robbery and rape. He was badly mistreated by other prisoners in his cell. They ate most of his food and poured food over his head and clothes. He was handcuffed and had metal rings fixed to both ankles that cut into his flesh. To add to his woes, he felt guilty for all he had done. He tried to commit suicide on several occasions. In desperation, the authorities transferred Huang to another cell. This cell contained some Christians who treated him in a very different way. His new cell mates were kind and sympathetic.

Yun, a Christian in the cell, talked to Huang in a kind way. They gave Huang extra portions from their own meagre rations of soup and food. This kindness reached his heart and he burst out crying. He exclaimed, "My brother, I am a murderer whom everyone hates. Even my father, mother, older and younger sister and fiancée don't want me. Why do you love me in this manner? There is no way I can repay you now, but after I die and turn into a ghost I will find some way to repay your goodness towards me."

Yun was then filled with a deep love for this young man and through his own tears said, "You should thank Jesus, for we believe in Him. If we didn't believe in Him, we would have treated you the same way as the prisoners in cell nine. Today we love you because of the love of Jesus Christ. Also, after you die not only can you not repay us, but your soul will enter eternal hell and punishment. Therefore you should repent and believe in Jesus because He is the only one able to save your soul."

Haung immediately and very sincerely said to the Lord, "Thank you Jesus, for loving a sinner like me."

Yun and the other Christians continued to care for Huang. They fed him, taught him the stories about Jesus, about His death and resurrection and second coming. They explained how he could get right with God. Huang wanted desperately to know more about the Bible. He lost his fear of death and came to love his Saviour very deeply.[50]

---

[50] Danyun, Lilies Amongst Thorns, Sovereign World 1991 p. 55–61

"That is all very nice," someone may say, "such love and forgiveness may have helped Huang, but are they real values, are they evidence based?" Instinctively we all value such characteristics, and we can show that statistically they can be helpful. However, without God they can only be artificial inventions fostered by man-made religions. We all know of placebo functions – could the Christian faith be put into that category? What a disaster it would be for someone to commit his or her life to following a lie. Yet if the Christian gospel is not true, what answers can we have for our society and ourselves? What will induce people to selflessly love others if there is no genuine creator who has selflessly loved them first? If the Christian story is true, what a disaster it is not to trust and follow Jesus Christ. The stakes are high! Values are valid because they are part of the very nature of our creator.

Many of the problems that we are facing in the west could be answered if we recognised the spiritual dimension of life that the Bible emphasises. Dying is not a tragedy if there is a heaven with a Saviour waiting for us there. Fraud and cheating, both at work and in relationships would be markedly reduced if we were sure that a Holy God is going to judge everything people think or do. The advantages are clear, yet how few understand that this is an essential area of study.

Many try to hide behind the label, 'agnostic' as if that has an aura of respectability. This word has the same root meaning as 'ignorant'. The Greek word 'gnosis' means knowledge, and the Greek prefixes 'a' and 'i' both mean 'without 'or 'not'. Could anyone successfully hide behind the label 'ignorant' in any other aspect of life when answers are there to be investigated?

A Chinese postgraduate student was talking about her interest in Christianity. She recognised that her country needed the values that Christianity brought with it. She has now realised that these values are not related to a religion but are the very nature of God himself, our creator. Jesus clearly demonstrated this. What her country needs is to be open to Jesus, the Lord of the universe. But first she needed to realise something vital. It is not just her society that needs Jesus. She needs him too. She needs the forgiveness he brings by paying for her sin himself on that cross. She needs the supernatural power he offers her, if she turns to Christ, to live this new life. It is not possible to live a Godly life, which will increasingly reveal these characteristics, unless we know that we have been forgiven, and have a longing to meet our Saviour later on. Living for Jesus Christ our Saviour becomes the greatest value we can have. All other values flow from him. She has now accepted the rule of Christ in her life.

Motives for Scepticism

Not only do people have emotional needs for God but we all have personal reasons why we want to reject him. If there is a God, he has the right to control how I should live! People must learn to be sceptical of their scepticism.

In the 1960s there was much publicity for the 'God is Dead' movement. In 1966, 'Time' magazine ran a headline on the front page, 'Is God Dead?' Since then many scholars started to show how shallow this view was. A few years later the same magazine's headline asked the question, "'Is God Coming Back to Life?"' In 1980, Time magazine ran a headline 'Modernising the Case for God.' In the article, they said, "In a quiet revolution in thought and argument that hardly anybody could have foreseen only two decades ago, God is making a comeback. Most intriguingly, this is happening not among theologians or ordinary believers, but in the crisp intellectual circles of academic philosophers, where consensus had long banished the Almighty from fruitful discourse."

In Tim Keller's book, *Making Sense of God*[51] he offers a description of the Christian life that is more robust and satisfying than secularism in many areas of life. It investigates what Keller calls 'the six givens of human life': meaning, satisfaction, freedom, identity, hope and justice. He presents a rational case for believing in God, and in the Christian God specifically. It is no surprise that today an increasing number of senior philosophers in universities are convinced Christians. It is by beginning with God that life makes sense.

Those who reject him always place a substitute idol in his place. It seems that my default setting puts me at the centre of everything. There are hardly any of my experiences in life that do not revolve around me.

We naturally think that it is in my best interests to swim with the tide and follow what the crowd thinks. Otherwise, how did the horror of anti-Semitism gain acceptance in Nazi Germany? If we are surrounded by people who reject God and his standards, it will be hard to swim against the tide. In nearly all the big decisions we make in life, will we go with the flow or swim against the current?

---

[51] Tim Keller, 'Making Sense of God,' Viking 2016

Chapter 6
'God Is, Therefore I Am'

The Bible begins with God, who has always existed. It emphasises that God is in control and that our thinking should centre on him. It teaches that there is one real God who has created a finite world into which he has placed man. The Bible begins,

"In the beginning God created the heavens and the earth." Genesis 1:1

This explains why our world is based on mathematics and laws. We call these laws the laws of Nature but the natural world of matter cannot create laws. The laws and rules that scientists see are the principles by which our creator has made this world. The basis of a rational world is a rational God. There can be no other explanation.

The Bible continues, Then God said, "Let us make man in our image, in our likeness, and let them rule." Genesis 1:26

This gives an explanation for the presence of our innate, moral, processing mind that works on a rational basis. Man has something of the mind of God.

World philosophies are based on one of two basic principles. One starts with God as our creator who has shared with us some of his attributes. The other starts with man at the centre with the possible concept of any God being derived from our thinking. It is no surprise that the latter approach has great trouble defining the source of rational, moral and aesthetic values within man, or of a rational mathematical world that we can investigate.

When there is a belief in a sovereign God, there are considerable consequences. It is notable that so many early scientists believed in a personal God. It was this belief that gave them the basis to investigate a world that they knew to be rational and worked according to God's laws. They could rely on their reason, because God had made man as a reasoning creation in a rational world.

It also explains why, when we turn against God and reject his right to rule, we also turn to selfish immorality and inhumanity. See what happens in atheistic states such as Stalin's and Putin's Russia, Hitler's Germany, Mao Tse tung's China, Pol Pot's Cambodia or North Korea today.

Jean-Jacques Rousseau (1712–1778)

Rousseau wrote in his book *Social Contract* about what he called his Copernicus discovery – that it is not God but man who is at the centre of the living universe. This thinking has been spreading rapidly ever since.

Paul Johnson, in his brilliant book *Intellectuals* has highlighted the effect man-centred philosophies have on the moral lives of such self-centred thinkers. He begins with Rousseau who felt he was not bound to live as others wanted and was consequently very egotistical. He admitted to being promiscuous, but he treated his consorts meanly. He had many children, the first five being abandoned nameless as soon as they were born. Two thirds of such babies died in the first year and only 14 per cent reached the age of seven but he didn't seem to care. His one-time friend David Hume said he was 'a monster who saw himself as the only important being in the universe'.

Most philosophers have recognised that there are inherent values that need to be accounted for. When the starting point for a philosophy is man in a material world, it has been hard to derive a strong basis for an inherent purpose to life and for values such as honesty, beauty and integrity to be real, in spite of the fact that nearly all humans recognise that these are core values that define humanity.

René Descartes (1596–1650)[52]

Descartes had a broad education under the Jesuits, typical for that time, studying classics, ethics, mathematics and theology. At university, he studied law but then became a soldier, becoming adept at riding and fencing. It was during his military training that his love of mathematics and logic came to the fore. His passion for trying to think about the larger questions of life then took over. He became involved with the Rosicrucian's, a secret order that sought to

---

[52] This brief summary owes much to E.W.F Tomlin's book, 'The Great Philosophers, the Western World' Skeffington and Son p 135–141

discover the 'mysterious esoteric truths of the ancient past', which 'concealed from the average man, provide insight into nature, the physical universe, and the spiritual realm.'[53] He began to be involved in meditation to try and discover these secrets. The Rosicrucian manifestos proclaimed a 'universal reformation of mankind', through a science allegedly kept secret for decades until the intellectual climate might receive it. Descartes was trying to discover answers from within himself.

On November 10th, 1619, whilst in a deeper meditative state than normal, he had a flash of inspiration which he felt opened up a completely new form of science. He then had a series of memorable dreams. In the first, he was lame and sought refuge in a church from a heavy storm. In the second, he was also in a violent storm with thunder and showers of sparks around him. In the third, he opened a book written by a Roman poet, Ausonius, (c. 310–c. 395 AD) where he read these words,

"Which way of life shall I follow?"

This experience had a profound effect on him. During the next eight years he spent much time meditating and seeking deeper truths. Although he remained a Roman Catholic, he did have an illegitimate son. He also wrote a treatise called *The World* in which he sided with Copernicus who had claimed that the earth was a planet and that the earth moves round the sun. Just at this time he heard of the way the Inquisition had condemned his contemporary, Galileo, for publishing similar ideas so he did not publish this as a book! However, he did publish the new ideas he had had since he had been meditating which resulted in the church authorities accusing him of atheism. Consequently, he fled to Sweden where he died a year later.

Although he always wanted to remain within the Roman Catholic church, he had strong feelings against its authoritarianism and the prescriptive way people were taught. He thought that ordinary people could find the truth for themselves without having to study the sacred texts and the eruditions of the scholars or follow the dictates of the pontiff. He felt that all ideas could be tested internally and that the truth would reveal itself by being 'clear and distinct' just as a mathematician determines the truth of a theorem. People must determine by constantly doubting and double checking any ideas presented to them.

---

[53] Martin, Pierre. Lodges, Orders and the Rosicross: Rosicrucianism in Lodges, Orders and Initiating Societies since the early 16th century. Edition Oriflamme, 2017.

His meditation and thinking led him to realise how imperfect he and his thinking processes were. He argued that seeing himself as imperfect meant that there must be a perfect being, there must be a God but this argument was later ridiculed by others, opening the door to atheistic philosophies that are also based on Descartes suppositions that start with man.

Descartes' thinking begins with himself. The fact that he could think led him to assume that he existed. He classically said, "I think, therefore I am."

By placing what, at first sight, seems reasonable, that man defines what is true, had far reaching consequences. It opened the doors to many subsequent philosophies, most of which accepted Descartes foundation that man is the judge of all things. Even the existence of God is brought before the mind of man to decide whether that concept is reasonable.

The tide was turning. Now it is God who is in the dock and man is the judge. Man is supreme and God, instead of being worshipped and obeyed, becomes the object of study. The difficulty is that it is impossible to put God under a finite microscope when he himself is infinite and we are definitely finite!

The scholar and writer, C.S. Lewis astutely analysed this tendency man always has to minimise his own sin and to place Almighty God in the dock, saying:

"The greatest barrier I have met is the almost total absence from the minds of my audience of any sense of sin. The early Christian preachers could assume in their hearers, whether Jews, Metuentes (God fearers), or Pagans, a sense of guilt. (That this was common among Pagans is shown by the fact that both Epicureanism and the mystery religions both claimed, though in different ways, to assuage it.) Thus, the Christian message was in those days unmistakably the Evangelium, the Good News. It promised healing to those who knew they were sick. We have to convince our hearers of the unwelcome diagnosis before we can expect them to welcome the news of the remedy. The ancient man approached God (or even the gods) as the accused person approaches his judge. For the modern man, the roles are quite reversed. He is the judge: God is in the dock. He is quite a kindly judge; if God should have a reasonable defence for being the god who permits war, poverty and disease, he is ready to listen to it. The trial may even end in God's acquittal. But the important thing is that man is on the bench and God is in the dock."[54]

---

[54] C.S. Lewis, God in the Dock: Essays on Theology and Ethics

It was Descartes who publicised this way of thinking, but ever since Adam, mankind has always tended to side-line and disregard God; at root this is what 'sin' is. A better maxim than Descartes would be 'God is – therefore I am.'

It is no coincidence that when God first revealed himself to Moses he puts himself at the centre when he said that his name was 'I am'!

'I am who I am.' Exodus 3:14

Immanuel Kant (1724–1804)

Kant was one of the most influential philosophers. He was raised in a strict Protestant home and with religious schooling, but he reacted against this. As a philosopher the basis of his thinking had man at the centre, 'human autonomy' was his key. He accepts that much of the data we live by comes into us by our senses but argued that a mass of chaotic sensations would not make sense without a pre-ordered mind which is somehow programmed to co-ordinate all the data. He argues that all that we consider to be true is dependent on the pre-ordered mind. He then goes on to suggest that everything that makes sense to us is because of this inherent mind that is programmed to make sense of everything. The mind, for him, is an active organ which co-ordinates all the sensations into ideas. He distinguishes sensations from perceptions. Sensations come via our senses of touch, taste, sight, smell and hearing through a vast network of nerves but these have to be sorted and made sense of by the mind. It is the mind that gives us perception of ideas. He tried to establish a basis for values and for God from this starting point.

Plato had spoken of 'the rabble of the senses' whereas Kant argued powerfully that that is all they would remain unless these sensations are ordered and sorted. We see this in modern computers. There are a wide variety of inputs but there has to be a core processor that is programmed to make sense of the data.

This mind, he suggests, is programmed to accept mathematics, space and time which are all necessary to make sense of the myriad of sensations we receive. So far this all makes sense.

Kant then argues that it is the mind that also transforms these 'perceptions' and converts them into 'conceptions' or ideas.

Kant felt that the philosopher Locke was wrong when he said, "There is nothing in the intellect except what is first in the senses," Leibnitz cleverly added, "nothing, except the intellect itself."

Kant tried to understand how moral values fit in. He claimed that the mind also contains 'an unanalysable feeling of the good' which supplies our moral obligations. But Kant doesn't say where this innate processing moral mind comes from!

The philosopher, Schopenhauer said, "Kant's greatest merit is the distinction of the phenomenon from the thing itself."

Kant didn't deny the existence of the real world outside of ourselves but suggests we can know nothing substantial about it.

On this basis, that all knowledge is subjective, how can we know for sure about God? Kant considers that all we know for sure is that space, time and cause and a moral sense are absolutes that are independent of our senses. Science becomes not an objective search for truth, but personally conceived ideas. His concept of the absolute is vague and gives rise to ideas such as 'This is my truth.' His ideas destroy true reality and undermine traditional doctrines such as a benevolent creator, an eternal soul with every man. As these ideas cannot be proved, religion becomes subjective and therefore cannot be denied. It is no wonder that clergymen in Germany in the later 18th century, who understood the consequences of Kant's thinking, protested so loudly against his views.

Although putting man, instead of God, at the starting point of our philosophy gives rise to many problems, the idea that implanted within us is a 'processor' or mind, that enables us to sort out and co-ordinate all the billions of sensations we receive, has much to support it. This innate processor does appear to have a moral sense, that we call a conscience. This could be the God-given source of the spiritual instincts that are in us all.

I have recently been asked if our brains are just made of neurons, synapses and chemical transmitters how do our minds differ from computers. The answer given in the Bible is that mankind is more than a machine. God did make man out of the dust of the earth, out of chemicals, but then he put his Spirit into man. It is because God has put his Spirit into us, we become both living and spiritual beings.

"The LORD God formed the man from the dust of the ground and breathed into his nostrils the breath of life, and the man became a living being." Genesis 2:7

Jean-Paul Sartre (1905–1980)

Sartre was a French writer and philosopher who lived in France during two world wars. He challenged the traditional ways of conformist living, he just wanted to live his own way. He had an inner dislike of 'bourgeoisie' lifestyles and thinking. He was an atheist and felt that people should be allowed to exist as they want and not as others want them to. 'Free will' meant he should be free to behave as he wanted to. Nobody else mattered. He popularised what came to be known as atheistic existentialism.

Although he rejected the concept of God, he did have a strong social conscience. He embraced Marxism but did not become a communist. He despised those who collaborated with the German occupation of France during the second World War but did not join the resistance. He was later awarded the Nobel prize for literature but refused to accept this.

He thought that, as God does not exist, the only person responsible for our behaviour is oneself. He concluded that humans were 'condemned to be free,' though he couldn't say who had condemned us. It must either be God or the thinking of humanity itself. He taught that there was no purpose in life but throughout his life he, illogically on his basis, thought that there were rights and wrongs, justice and injustices.

Sartre tried to take the idea that man is the centre of everything, that previous philosophers such as Descartes and Kant had espoused, and he showed the emptiness and meaningless of the life that this inevitably results in. Existentialists have no means of explaining how mankind has inherent principles and values, how these should be developed and why we feel life has a purpose when there can be none, according to their thinking.

Without God man is lost, without purpose and without knowing definitely how to behave. We have no foundation on which to build our lives.

Ancient Christian Thinkers

It is remarkable that so many of the notable Christian philosophers recognised that our thinking must begin with God if we are to make sense of life and not be nihilistic.

Augustine 354–430 AD wrote, "Believe that you may understand" (Crede ut intelligas). He recognised that faith and reason were interdependent.

Anselm 1033–1109 AD wrote, "I believe I order that I might understand" (Crede ut intelligam), emphasising that God must be the basis for reason and understanding.

Thomas Aquinas 1225–1274 wrote, "I understand and I believe" (Intelligo et credo). He recognised that some truths are discovered by reason acting on faith but other truths must come directly from revelation. He saw that even our reason is limited and is biased by our natural sin.[55]

The Bible's Answer to Man-Centred Philosophies

It is highly significant that the Bible begins with God who created the universe and then put man on earth. It is only by beginning with God that life can make sense.

"In the beginning God created the heavens and the earth." Genesis 1:1

"Then God said, let us make man in our image, in our likeness and let them rule." Genesis 1:26

God determined that there should always be people who would live according to God's wishes and so fulfil his aims. God taught this people,

"Hear, O Israel: **The LORD our God** is one, the LORD is one." Deuteronomy 6:4

We were made to live under the authority of our creator. He continues,

"Love **the LORD your God** with all your heart and with all your soul and with all your strength. These commandments I give you today are to be upon your hearts. Impress them upon your children. Talk about them when you sit at home." Deuteronomy 6:4–7

Such thinking is the opposite of the famous dictum by the poet Swinburne who, mocking the angelic host, wrote,

"Glory to man in the highest for man is the master of things."

Even God's people have a strong tendency to drift away from a close relationship with God. When Joshua had led God's people into the promised land, he reminded them of all that God had done for them but then added that they must make a decision about who is going to be sovereign, themselves, the gods around them or the LORD himself.

---

[55] Summary by Kenneth Richard Samples in 'Christianity Cross-Examined' Reasons to Believe, Covina, 2021 p.63

"Now fear the LORD and serve him with all faithfulness. Throw away the gods your forefathers worshipped and serve the LORD. But if serving the LORD seems undesirable to you, then choose for yourselves this day whom you will serve, whether the gods your forefathers served or the Gods of the Amorites, in whose land you are living. But as for me and my household, we will serve the LORD." Joshua 24:14–15

Isaiah, who died around 681 BC, recognised that there were essentially just two ways of thinking. He concluded that people will either allow God to be at the centre of their lives or they will provide themselves with their own lights, but this latter group will face tragic consequences. He also understood that there can be pseudo-faith where people say they trust in God but do not obey or rely on him in practice.

"Who among you fears the LORD and obeys the word of his servant? Let him who walks in the dark, who has no light, trust in the name of the LORD and rely on his God. But now, all you who light fires and provide yourselves with flaming torches, go, walk in the light of your fires and of the torches you have set ablaze. This is what you shall receive from my hand: You will lie down in torment." Isaiah 50:10–11

Jeremiah also noted that it was man, wanting his independence from God, that is the root cause of our problems.

"My people have committed two sins: they have forsaken me, the spring of living water and have dug their own cisterns that cannot hold water." Jeremiah 2:13

When mankind, represented by Adam and Eve, walked with God in the Garden of Eden they had both purpose and joy. When they rejected God, they lost both. Humanity now has the option to return to live under the authority of God who has now revealed himself in the person of Jesus. By his own death, Jesus has enabled us again to live in partnership with our creator because he has taken on himself the penalty and consequences of our sins.

One of the great Messianic psalms looks forwards to the day when the Messiah, God's chosen king, would enter his world,

"Your throne, O God, will last for ever and ever; a sceptre of justice will be the sceptre of your kingdom. You love righteousness and hate wickedness; therefore God, your God, has set you above your companions by anointing you with the oil of joy." Psalm 45:6–7

John the Baptist experienced this same joy because he lived under the authority of God. He saw his life as being fulfilled by being in a relationship with his Lord and Saviour. He said, "I am not the Christ but am sent ahead of him. The bride belongs to the bridegroom. The friend who attends the bridegroom waits and listens for him and is full of joy when he hears the bridegroom's voice. That joy is mine and is now complete. He must become greater; I must become less." John 3:28–30

The apostle Paul also turned to live under the authority of God. He then understood that purpose, satisfaction and truth can only be found together in the person of God's Messiah. He concluded,

"For me to live is Christ and to die is gain." Philippians 1:21

The Bible teaches that this world is just a trial run. The real world is the one to come where we will live in full harmony with our creator. That is what Jesus has promised us, that is what the whole Bible speaks about.

A schoolboy made a poignant mistake in an essay he had written. He should have described Jesus as 'God's only begotten Son' but instead he wrote, "God's only forgotten son." People have forgotten that it is only by beginning with God that life makes sense.

Chapter 7
Contemporary Witnesses to Jesus

Dr E.V. Rieu translated Homer for the Penguin Classics series. He had been an agnostic all his life. He was then asked to translate the four gospels for the same series. When his son heard of this, he commented,

"It's going to be interesting to see what father will do with the four gospels, and it's going to be more interesting to see what the four gospels will do to father."

He did not have to wait very long. Within one year, E.V. Rieu responded to the evidence he saw in the gospels; he became a committed Christian and joined a church. He subsequently sat on the committee that produced the New English Bible.

John wrote his gospel to convince people about Jesus. He recorded key evidence, much as a barrister selects what evidence to present to a court to convince a judge and jury. It is worth remembering the key verses he puts towards the end of his gospel.

"Jesus did many other miraculous signs in the presence of his disciples, which are not recorded in this book. But **these are written that you may believe that Jesus is the Christ, the Son of God, and that by believing you may have life in his name**." John 20:30–31

In John chapter 5, Jesus selects some witnesses to support his claim, made earlier in the chapter, to be one with God his Father. Jesus has already had his say about who he is, but he acknowledges that his testimony alone is not enough. As Mark Twain wrote in another context,

"His saying so doesn't make it so. "[56]

So Jesus calls up other witnesses.

---

[56] Mark Twain, 'Tom Sawyer', chapter I, page 4

The Evidence of John, the Baptist

John appeared, unannounced, and started to preach, in the inhospitable desert, about what God sees in people's hearts. Outward religion was not enough for God, a public repentance and a personal turning back to the Lord is essential and this change can be sealed by public baptism. People recognised that his was the voice of God and vast numbers responded to his shining light – at least temporarily.

"John was a lamp that burned and gave light, and you chose, for a time to enjoy his light." John 5:35

However, the main message of John was to prepare the way for God's Messiah.

"…but the reason I came baptising with water was that he might be revealed to Israel…I have seen and **testify that this is the Son of God**." John 1:31

But as so often happens John and his message were rejected. Herod Antipas arrested John the Baptist, because John had publicly opposed the affair that Herod was having with his brother's wife. This resulted in John being imprisoned and then beheaded. When leaders reject the truth, other people usually follow.

In the eighteenth century, London and all England were stirred by the preaching of John and Charles Wesley and George Whitfield, much as John the Baptist's preaching had affected first century Israel. When he was young, John Wesley, being an ordained Anglican minister, was invited to preach in London churches. However, after preaching in St Helen's Bishopsgate, he was told, in no uncertain way, by the Church Wardens,

"Sir, you must preach here no more."

If you read the histories of London in the eighteenth century, it is striking that the revival ministries of Wesley's and Whitefield are hardly mentioned. Historians were selective according to their own prejudices.

For a time, people rejoiced in the light of John the Baptist but then they turned back to their old ways. They realised the implications of this teaching and found this hard. The evidence was there but they rejected it.

The Evidence of the Miracles

The major prophets in the Old Testament had performed some miracles but no-one had or would ever replicate what Jesus did.

"I have a testimony that is weightier than that of John. **For the very work that my father has given me to finish**, and that which I am doing, testifies that the Father has sent me." John 5:36

Already in John's gospel several of these miracles have been alluded to. When Nicodemus, a ruler of Israel who sat on the Sanhedrin Council, came to meet Jesus his opening line was,

"Rabbi, we know that you are a teacher who comes from God. **For no one could do the miraculous signs you are doing if God were not with him**." John 3:2

There are thirty-three separate miracles that Jesus performed that are recorded in the gospels but John tells us that he did many more. A miracle occurs when the laws of nature are broken. God does cause coincidences to happen but strictly these are not miracles. In the Old Testament, one of the features of God's coming Messiah would be his ability to perform astounding miracles. Isaiah talks about what will happen when God himself will come to his earth,

"Then the eyes of the blind will be opened and the ears of the deaf unstopped. Then will the lame leap like a deer, and the mute tongue shout for joy." Isaiah 35:5

Jesus did fulfil all these prophecies, both physically but also figuratively; the spiritually blind and spiritually deaf came to see and hear what God had come to do. Jesus had just mentioned his ability to 'give life' to people.

"I tell you the truth, whoever hears my word and believes him who sent me, has eternal life and will not be condemned; he has crossed over from death to life." John 5:24

Life was considered as a gift that only God can give to inanimate matter. When Jesus was on earth, he raised four people from the dead. He raised the widow's son in the village of Nain (Luke 7:15), the 12–year-old daughter of Jairus, a ruler of a synagogue (Mark 5:42), and Lazarus, the brother of Mary and Martha in Bethany after he had been dead four days (John 11:44). Finally he himself was raised from the dead after he had been crucified. He had repeatedly told his disciples that three days after his death he would rise again.

The miracles Jesus enacted are important evidence. Jesus said later to his disciples that unbelief was irrational,

"He who hates me hates my Father as well. If I had not done among them what no-one else did, they would not be guilty of sin. **But now they have seen these miracles, and yet they have hated both me and my Father**. But this was to fulfil what is written in their Law; 'They hated me without reason'." John 15:25

The Evidence of God Himself

There is some debate about the meaning of the next argument Jesus uses:

"And the Father who sent me **has himself testified concerning me**. You have never heard his voice." John 5:37

This could refer to the proclamation the Father made when Jesus began his public ministry, when he was baptised by John the Baptist:

"And a voice came from heaven: '**You are my Son**, whom I love; with you I am well pleased'." Mark 1:11

This declaration was to be repeated when Jesus was transfigured into a dazzling being in the presence of Moses and Elijah on top of a high mountain. Peter, James and John witnessed this and heard a voice from the cloud clearly saying,

"This is my Son, whom I love. Listen to him." Mark 9:7

An alternative view is that God spoke through the Scriptures, as Jesus continues,

"…nor does **his word dwell in you**, for you do not believe the one he sent." John 5:38

The Evidence of Scripture

In Jesus' time, there were many religious Jews who scrupulously studied the Scriptures but somehow, they had missed what the Scriptures were talking about. They are all about God's Chosen King who was to come into his world – His Messiah.

The Jewish Rabbis were meticulous in their copying and studying the Scriptures, which are now our Old Testament. Copyists would only copy one letter at a time before going back to the original, just to be sure no mistakes were made. They would check the central letter of each line and each book.

The highly esteemed Rabbi, Hillel made the interesting observations,

"More flesh – more worms

More wealth – more carefully

More maidservants – more lewdness

More menservants – more thieving

More women – more witchcraft

There was one thing he did value,

More Torah – more life."

Hillel went on,

"Whosoever has gained a good name has gained it for himself, Whosoever has gained the words of the Torah has gained for himself life in the world to come."

A similar thinking is seen amongst some Muslims who consider that learning the Qur'an by heart will put them in good stead with God. Such people associate knowledge of the Scriptures with salvation.

A group of school children were taken to the Boijmans Van Beuningen Museum in Rotterdam. They trooped into a room with paintings by Rubens. The children started to criticise the pictures and discussed all that they considered to be wrong, 'The hands are too big, no one smiles like that, the colours aren't real and so on'. After a while, the curator could stand this no more and he went up to the teacher in charge and said,

"Please could you explain to the children that it is not the Rubens pictures that are being judged here, it is the visitors."

There is great power in the words of the Bible to change people – but only if we see our need, are willing to be changed, and submit to the Saviour the Bible talks about. If we, like those children in the art museum, think we are superior, then we can gain nothing from God's words. This is what Moses said to God's chosen people of old,

"Take this book of the Law and place it besides the ark of the covenant of the LORD your God. **There it will remain as a witness against you**. For I know how rebellious and stiff necked you are. If you have been rebellious against the LORD while I am still alive and with you, how much more will you rebel after I die." Deuteronomy 31:26–27

Many homes have a Bible somewhere on their bookshelves. In Victorian times, most families would have a large Family Bible but this was usually just used to record births, deaths, and to press flowers. Yet the Bible tells us how our relationship with God can be restored by Jesus, God's Messiah.

All of God's people should be Bible students, should work to understand it, and learn sections by heart. Without such dedication we cannot progress as Christians. Dr Harry Ironside became Minister of Moody Church in Chicago. He had no college education yet became the foremost Bible teacher in his generation. From his biography, we learn,

"Under his mother's guidance, Harry began to memorise Scripture from the age of 3. By the age of 14, he had read through the Bible 14 times, once for each year of his life. During the rest of his life he read the Bible through at least once each year."

On one occasion, he was speaking at a conference and he and a fellow speaker began to discuss their own devotional life. The other speaker said what he had been reading from the Bible that morning and he then asked Harry Ironside when he had read. At first, he was hesitant, but then he said,

"I read the book of Isaiah!"

He was saturated with the word of God. This is true for most of the great Bible teachers. John Bunyan, who wrote Pilgrim's Progress spent 12 years in Bedford prison for refusing to stop preaching the word of God. He had little formal education but it was said of him,

"Cut him and you will find his blood is Bibline."

Everything John Bunyan did was steeped in the Bible. The point of Scripture is to show us our deep needs and to point us to the only Saviour our creator has provided.

The agnostic scholar, who became a Christian, E.V. Rieu, concluded about the Bible,

'These words bear the seal of the Son of Man and of God, and they are the Magna Carta of the human spirit.'

The Evidence of Our Hearts

God knows what is really important for each of us. He is not interested in the volume of our verbal praise of him. The only worship he accepts is hearts that are genuinely devoted to him.

"I do not accept praise from men, but I know you. **I know that you do not have the love of God in your hearts**." John 5:41–42

The Bible students of Jesus' day were much more concerned to be recognised by fellow scholars that to be recognised by God. The way they dressed, talked and performed their outward religion was all to impress people – they weren't so concerned about pleasing God. Yet their Scriptures emphasised that true worship should always be the purpose of life.

A headteacher was addressing the pupils in his school on their speech day. He rightly said, "The purpose of life is to discover the purpose of life and then to make that the purpose of your life."

The Jewish Confession of faith, the Shema, taken from what God said to Moses, explains the priority of life,

"Hear, O Israel: The LORD our God, the LORD is one. Love the LORD you God with all your heart and with all your soul and with all your strength." Deuteronomy 6:4–5

What God wants is nothing less than our hearts. A missionary to some tribespeople in the Amazon attended a tribal meeting. The chief stood up and said,

"I am impressed with Jesus. I want to give him a gift of some money."

The missionary then told the group that God does not need our gifts. The Chief thought again and said,

"I am so impressed with Jesus that I want to give him my youngest wife!"

Again, the missionary explained that this was not what God required. The light then dawned on the Chief,

"I now understand. God wants my heart, then I give myself to Jesus because he is God."

The decision we make over who controls our life should not be an arbitrary one, based on my personal desires, it should be based on evidence, just as Jesus insisted that people should make up their minds about his claims based on the evidence.

Chapter 8
Further Evidence Given by Jesus

Aleksei Navalny, the Russian strongly opposed to Russian President Vladimir Putin and his government, has served many jail sentences for organising protest rallies that have been mainly directed against government corruption. In October 2018, he was publicly challenged to a duel by Putin's long-time Security Chief, Viktor Zolotov. This challenge was made in a video, with Zolotov appearing in full uniform with cap and epaulets. He claimed that whatever weapon was chosen by Navalny, he would 'make mincemeat of him'. Navalny accepted the challenge, but the weapon he chose was to be a live television debate. The duel has not taken place!

Jesus was also considered to be a public enemy by the Jewish rulers and they wanted to find ways to get rid of him. In John 8:48–59, the Jews engage Jesus in a public debate, that had all the features of a verbal duel. Jesus had just told the Jewish authorities that the reason they do not hear God speaking to them was because they are not God's people – they did not belong to God.

They respond very aggressively with two aggressive statements,

"Aren't we right in saying that **you are a Samaritan** and **demon possessed**." John 8:48

Jesus, without calling them names, repeats the truths he has so frequently made previously.

"I am not possessed by a demon,' said Jesus, 'but I honour my Father and you dishonour me." John 8:49

Then they attack again,

"Now we know that you are demon possessed!" John 8:52

In response, Jesus restated his divine claims but then accuses his attackers of dishonesty. The effect was that the authorities wanted to stone Jesus to death there and then, but Jesus managed to slip away. There is much to learn from the details of this dialogue which is the climax of the previous two chapters.

Jesus had set the scene for what was to come when he made a public proclamation in the Court of Women of the Temple in Jerusalem. This court was bathed in light during the Feast of Tabernacles from four massive lamps. He cried out,

"I am the light of the world. Whoever follows me will never walk in darkness but will have the light of life." John 8:12

Jesus claims that he alone is the key to understanding life. This theme of light shining is the basis for what John subsequently selected for his book. Chapter 8 makes the claims of Jesus abundantly clear. At the beginning of chapter 9, Jesus heals a man who had been born blind. This story is surely inserted here to highlight the blindness of the religious leaders who were opposed to God's truth and that Jesus alone can enable them to see. It is all part of John's thesis that 'light is shining in the darkness'. (John 1:5).

The Claims of Jesus

Jesus then emphasises two statements in this passage. These are clearly very important because they both begin with,

"I tell you the truth…"

They summarise the message of the whole Bible. The first is,

"I tell you the truth, if anyone keeps **my** word, **he will never see death**." John 8:51

This teaches what Jesus had come to achieve, although it is put in a negative form. Jesus has come that we 'may have life and have it to the full' (John 10:10), he came that we might never see death.

The second is,

"I tell you the truth…**before Abraham was born, 'I am!'**" John 8:58

This teaches who Jesus claimed to be. He is saying that Abraham looked forwards to his day.

A person who understands and fully accepts these two statements is a Christian, they are the basis for experiencing 'life to the full'.

Let us look at these two verses in more detail.

1. **"If anyone keeps my word he will never see death"** John 8:51

The word 'death' has three meanings in Scripture. It can mean the physical dissolution of our bodies at the end of this present life.

Death also is used to refer to that ultimate disaster when we leave this world without the forgiveness Christ offers to meet God the judge and to be dismissed from his presence forever.

"But for the cowardly and unbelieving and abominable and murderers and immoral persons and sorcerers and idolaters and all liars, their part will be in the lake that burns with fire and brimstone, **which is the second death**." Revelation 21:8

Thirdly, death can also mean our alienation from God before we find forgiveness in Christ. Thus, Paul wrote,

"As for you, **you were dead** in your transgressions and sins." Ephesians 2:1

"When you were **dead in your sins**." Colossians 2:13

We need to distinguish which death Jesus is talking about. In this context, Jesus clearly cannot be talking about physical death as all his disciples would die physically. Later John brings the different meanings of death together when Jesus comforts Mary and Martha after the death of his friend Lazarus,

Jesus said to her, "I am the resurrection and the life. **He who believes in me will live, even though he dies**." John 11:25

The following verse adds another meaning, eternal death,

"...and **whoever lives and believes in me will never die**. Do you believe that?" John 11:26

Note these final words, "Do you believe that?" are left out in the liturgy of funeral services. It is usual at funerals for the minister to walk down the aisle in front of the coffin, surrounded by people who may not normally go to church, but it might be helpful if the minister could add these words that are in the original text, and, whilst looking around at everyone, ask them,

"Do you believe that?"

Their eternal destiny does depend on their response.

When the great evangelist D. L. Moody was about to die, he said confidently to those around him,

"Earth is receding, heaven is approaching. This is my crowning day."

Christian funerals should be a mixture of triumph overcoming the natural sadness – contrast their joy with the atmosphere at atheist or humanist funerals.

"Where, O death is your victory? Where, O death, is your sting? But thanks be to God. He gives us the victory through our Lord Jesus Christ." 1 Corinthians 15:55–56

Jesus is absolutely clear when talking to his opponents, that if any will believe in him, will follow him, will let his word be their guide then they will never see death, they will never be separated from the God who made them and who died to save them.

During this discussion Jesus makes yet another claim to be the one and only son of God.

"My father, whom you claim as your God, is the one who glorifies me. Though you do not know him, I know him. If I said I did not, I would be a liar like you, but I do know him and keep his word." John 8:54–55

There could be no confusion now. He is saying that his Father is the God of the Old Testament, and he is adamant that this is the truth. Jesus had never and would never say anything untrue, so he throws down the gauntlet. The proof that he is God's Son is that he always does what his heavenly Father says.

As this chapter was being written the television and newspapers were full of the manifestos of those who want to be the next Prime Minister. Here Jesus is putting forwards his manifesto that begins with what he longs to bring about. For him nuclear war is not the ultimate disaster, it is for us to face eternal death; to enter eternity unprepared to meet God; to die and wake up the other side knowing that there is no more hope. This is Christ's manifesto, he wants to save us from hell for heaven, so this should be the manifesto of his church. Why are our churches so embarrassed about passing on this manifesto about heaven and hell and the only Saviour? Our message should be that any person who follows Christ, and who lives by Christ's word, will never face the tragedy of hell.

2. "I tell you the truth…Before Abraham was born, 'I am!" John 8:51

This is the other main point in Jesus' manifesto.

The grammar here seems to be all wrong, 'before Abraham was, I am!' The answer is to be found in the Old Testament. When the Lord God met Moses at the 'burning bush' and told Moses to be his representative in freeing the children of Israel from their captivity in Egypt, Moses asked how he was to explain this to the Israelites,

"Suppose I go to the Israelites and say to them, 'The God of your Fathers has sent me to you' and they ask me 'what is his name?' Then what shall I tell them?'" God said to Moses, "I AM WHO I AM." This is what you are to say to the Israelites: "**I AM' has sent me to you**." Exodus 3:13–14

Jesus is clearly referring to this account and is claiming to be the same God as the one the Jews debating with him were claiming to follow. The Jews clearly understood what Jesus was saying; it is made eloquently clear by the sentence that follows,

"At this, they picked up stones to stone him." John 8:59

It was blasphemy for a man to claim to be God. What was missing was a fair investigation of the charge against Jesus.

It is staggering that, in spite of this immense claim by Jesus, there is a complete lack of self-seeking by him.

"I am not seeking glory for myself." John 8:50

"If I glorify myself, my glory means nothing. My Father, whom you claim as your God, is the one who glorifies me." John 8:54

How many of the world's politicians could honestly say that they are simply doing what God wants? How many would be willing to die for what they say they believe in? Jesus is surely the light shining in our darkness.

The Message of the Church

Jesus is saying, "I am one with the eternal God. I have come to earth to bring this news of salvation to you. I have come to give your life, both now and in eternity. If anyone keeps my word, he will never see death."

Jesus is saying that anyone can avoid being separated from God eternally by really accepting these two claims. Jesus can only save us, by taking responsibility for our sin, if he really is who he claims to be. If he is not God, he cannot be our Saviour. They must stand together. These are all extraordinary claims and yet there is so much evidence to support them.

Today many think that a Christian education is to help children to become nice, kind pleasant members of society. That is not the Christian message, it is far too limited, even though this may be a spin off. Why are we so ashamed to pass on what Jesus teaches?

People will want to know how they can change for the better and experience the power of the Spirit to change them into becoming like Jesus. Just telling people to be good will never bring about this change.

A headmaster wrote the following in his autobiography, "I was happy in conversation with boys always to tell them what ideal behaviour was and where selfishness, cruelty and exploitation lay but unwilling to talk of the very centre of Christianity, the meaning of the cross because I found it at times repugnant and in part beyond belief. With this semi-religion, I was able to live with some contentment, but I knew well that it was 'non-infectious. That if what I believed was all Christianity amounted to, it would attract few. I knew that our Lord did not walk about Palestine beginning a world revolution, by saying, "Come along everyone, be nice to everybody, be truthful, be honest. No, he spoke of repentance, of salvation from sin, of conversion."

How right this headmaster is. The Christian message is that the Spirit of Jesus, the Spirit of God, is at work. He enables us to recognise our rebellion against God, and draws us to Jesus Christ, the Saviour of any who turn to him. When we respond, his Spirit enters our life and begins the radical change in our characters. The Holy Spirit wants us to become like Jesus.

The Darkness

Jesus claims that many are living in great spiritual darkness and John illustrates this by the reaction of the Jewish leaders. Note the characteristics of those who oppose him.

1. Anger

They lapse into irrational even vitriolic anger,

The Jews answered him, "Are we right in saying that you are a Samaritan and demon possessed?" John 8:48

Such slurs are quoted in all four gospels. In Mark's gospel we read,

"And the teachers of the law who came down from Jerusalem said, "He is possessed by Beelzebub. By the prince of demons he is driving our demons." Mark 3:22

On that occasion, Jesus answered the irrational attack. He argues that if a king is fighting himself, he must lose! In the same way, a household in which the husband and wife are constantly fighting will be destroyed. Jesus is saying that it is irrational and absurd to think that he is driving out Satan by the power of Satan. It is darkness that is irrational and spiteful, God is recognised by truth and love.

2. Lying

Darkness is also characterised by dishonesty. Satan is the father of lies. Jesus picks this up,

"Though you do not know him, I know him. If I said I did not I would be **a liar like you**, but I do know him and keep his word." John 8:55

Those, in whom God has put his Spirit, also know God and this will be seen in the way they speak the truth with love.

3. Ignorance of God

Have you noticed how often politicians who are being interviewed and are facing a difficult question will begin their answer with,

'Now the fact is…' or 'We all know…' or 'To tell you the truth…'

Although the Jewish leaders knew and understood so little about Jesus, they said,

"Aren't we right in saying…" John 8:48

Yet they were clearly wrong. Then they said,

"Now we know…" John 8:52

Yet they were 'clearly ignorant' if they really thought that Jesus could conceivably be demon possessed.

Later the Jews confronted the man born blind, that Jesus had healed. We read,

"Then they **hurled insults** at him and said, 'You are this fellow's disciple! We are disciples of Moses! We know that God spoke to Moses, but as for this fellow, **we don't even know where he comes from**." John 9:28–29

The man answered using irony,

"Now that is remarkable! **You don't know** where he comes from, yet he opened my eyes. **We know** that God does not listen to sinners. He listens to the godly man who does his will. Nobody has ever heard of opening the eyes of a man born blind. If this man were not from God, he could do nothing." John 9:30–33

Such understanding was met with further ridicule and opposition. They said to the man,

"You were steeped in sin at birth; how dare you lecture us! And they threw him out." John 9:34

Summary

Jesus claims to be God's light shining in the darkness, yet the darkness betrays itself in the way it reacts to the light.

The prime issue

The issue at stake is the person of Jesus. John focuses on 'glory' in verse 54 quoted below, but the issue was not the glory of God, that was not questioned, but the 'glory' of Jesus, and this is what his father is trying to establish.

"I am not seeking glory for myself, **but there is one who seeks it, and he is the judge**." John 8:50

There are many religious leaders in the world who claim that God is their God yet they also fail to glory in Jesus.

"My Father, whom you claim as your God, is the one who glorifies me." John 5:54

The wording here is fascinating. The Jew's authority is their claim to follow their God and yet their God excludes the true Son of God. It seems they had a different God. Their demeanour, their anger and spitefulness betray that they are not following the God of love of the Bible, who is slow to anger!

In the modern world, there is a feeling that all religions are essentially similar and are there to give people an ethic to live by and a purpose to live for. We should be saying to them, as Jesus said to religious people of his day,

"You claim to worship God but are you pointing people to me?"

One of the marks of the faith the real creator God wants to see in us is that he points people to Jesus, so that men may glory in him and be changed by receiving his Spirit when they turn to him. True religion gives people a confidence that they have been put right with God, who then empowers them to live for him.

The average man, even if a churchgoer, doesn't glory in Jesus and is not being changed by him. However, God seeks to glorify his Son, Jesus, and so do all those who are members of the Kingdom of God.

Is there a middle way?

Can people not try to live good lives but reject Jesus? The Bible is clear, they can try to do that but it can never put them right with God. The vital point is that no-one can be good enough for God. Being sincerely religious does not impress God. We are either forgiven, and this can only be found in Jesus, or we are still responsible for our own sin. This will be apparent when we die and meet God. We are either members of the Kingdom of God or outside it – there is no middle way, as far as God is concerned. Either Jesus is demon possessed or he is the Son of God.

Too many people are willing to accept Jesus as a great moral teacher but refuse to accept his claim to be God. C. S. Lewis, wrote powerfully in his book *Mere Christianity*,

"I am trying here to prevent anyone saying the really foolish thing that people often say about Him: I'm ready to accept Jesus as a great moral teacher, but I don't accept his claim to be God. That is the one thing we must not say. A man who was merely a man and said the sort of things Jesus said would not be a great moral teacher. He would either be a lunatic – on the level with the man who says he is a poached egg – or else he would be the Devil of Hell. You must make your choice."

In John chapter 8, there is no thought of Jesus being a great moral teacher, it was his claim to be God that was the focus of discussion.

"**Are you greater than our father Abraham**? He died and so did the prophets. **Who do you think you are?**" John 8:53

Any who reject Jesus' claim have to conclude, with the Jews, that somehow, he is of the devil.

In 1936, Watchman Nee, the great Chinese Bible teacher and evangelist, made a similar argument in his book *Normal Christian Faith*, saying that a person who claims to be God must belong to one of three categories:

"First, if he claims to be God and yet in fact is not, he has to be a madman or a lunatic.

Second, if he is neither God nor a lunatic, he has to be a liar, deceiving others by his lie.

Third, if he is neither of these, he must be God.

You can only choose one of the three possibilities.

If you do not believe that he is God, you have to consider him a madman.

If you cannot take him for either of the two, you have to take him for a liar.

There is no need for us to prove if Jesus of Nazareth is God or not. All we have to do is find out if He is a lunatic or a liar. If He is neither, He must be the Son of God."

How often people will say,

"Yes, I would call myself a Christian, I was baptised, but I'm not the practising sort!"

Such people need to be warned that if they drift from Christ they have drifted from the only hope of salvation that there is.

Who knows for certain?

Clearly there is one person who knows the truth about Jesus and that person is the very definition of truth, God himself. By raising Jesus from the dead, he revealed what he thought of Jesus and his teaching. At Peter's Pentecost sermon, it was made clear that the cross demonstrated what man thought of God's Son, Jesus whilst the empty grave demonstrated what God thought of his Son.

It is all too easy to miss what is valuable. Off the shores of the Philippines a fisherman discovered a large misshapen pearl. It was not very attractive, looking like a giant amoeba with blobs and folds everywhere. He took the unusual find home and stored it under his bed. Ten years later he moved and, having no use for it, gave it to the local tourism office. It turned out to be the world's largest pearl with an estimated value of approximately 100 million dollars. It is so easy to miss the value of something if it is not what we are looking for.

The decision we make about Jesus has immense consequences both for our lives here on earth but also, importantly, for eternity.

Chapter 9
Old Testament Prophecies

This brings us to another group of stepping stones. The Bible teaches that the God, who created this world, knows what will happen in the future and sometimes tells us about these in some astonishing prophecies.

Again and again people, and especially God's people, are warned that if they fail to live with and for the one true God he will eventually become angry and exert his judgment and wrath on them. It also stresses God's faithfulness to those who follow him. Zephaniah was a prophet in the days of King Josiah (640–609 BC). He prophesied the complete destruction of the great city of Nineveh and other states that surrounded Israel. It is astounding that, of all those nations, it is the Jews who remain a distinct people.

The book of Daniel was written during the Babylonian captivity of the Jews in the sixth century BC. It contains some remarkable prophecies about the subsequent Persian, Greek and Roman dynasties. Daniel foresees the coming of a Messiah, a man, who would be equal to God himself, who would be worshipped by people throughout the world and whose kingdom will be eternal. This was an astounding claim for a Jew to make.

"In my vision at night, I looked, and there before me was one like a son of man, coming with the clouds of heaven. He approached the Ancient of Days and was led into his presence. **He was given authority, glory and sovereign power; all peoples, nations and men of every language worshipped him. His dominion is an everlasting dominion** that will not pass away, and **his kingdom is one that will never be destroyed.**" Daniel 7:1314

It is this kingdom that Jesus introduced and that is still growing.

The Messiah's Ancestry

The whole of the Old Testament looks forwards to the coming of the Messiah, a future Jewish king from the line of King David, who was expected to rule God's people eternally. His coming is first mentioned right at the beginning of the book of Genesis when Satan is warned that a descendant of Eve would crush his power. The Lord God says,

"And I will put enmity between you and the woman, and between your offspring and hers; he will crush your head and you will strike his head." Genesis 3:15

The story continues to explain how God chose a man from Ur, Abraham, to be the Father of a great nation, the people of God, and from this nation the Messiah was to come.

"I will make you into a great nation and I will bless you; I will make your name great and you will be a blessing. I will bless those who bless you, and whoever curses you will curse; and **all peoples of the earth will be blessed through you**." Genesis 12:3

Abraham was told that he and his wife, Sarah, would have a son in their old age who would continue their line. Isaac was eventually born. Yet later Abraham was told to sacrifice this son, whom God had said would be his successor! He therefore took his Son up to Mount Moriah to offer this sacrifice but the Lord intervened at the last minute and provided a ram as a substitute. Mount Moriah was later renamed to become, very significantly, the Temple Mount in Jerusalem where symbolic sacrifices were to be offered for the sins of God's people. This was surely a visual prophecy of what the Messiah, a descendant of Abraham and Isaac, would eventually achieve.

Isaac had twins, Esau and Jacob. It was the younger one, Jacob, that God chose to continue the line until the coming of the Messiah. The older son, Esau became the father of the Edomites, the person whose descendants became antagonistic to the Jews. God later met with Jacob and he was told,

"Your descendants will be like the dust of the earth, and you will spread out to the west and to the east, to the north and to the south. All peoples of the earth will be blessed **through you and your offspring**. I am with you and will watch over you wherever you go." Genesis 28:14–15

The tantalising question is which offspring is meant. The Lord then changed Jacob's name to 'Israel' which means 'Wrestled with God.'

The Bible includes an extraordinary story in Genesis 38 concerning Judah who had twins with his daughter-in-law Tamar, when she had pretended to be a prostitute. Why was this sordid story included? The reason is that one of these sons was a man called Peres. So what? We read in later genealogies that Perez was to be in the direct ancestral line of the coming Messiah (See Ruth 4:18 and Matthew 1:3)

The Jews went down to Egypt after Joseph, one of Isaacs twelve sons, became Viceroy of Egypt. Before Jacob died, he called his twelve sons to him and spoke to each. It was to Judah that he said,

"The sceptre will not depart from Judah, nor the rulers staff from beneath his feet **until he comes to whom it belongs and the obedience of the nations is his**." Genesis 49:10

Who is this looking forwards to? Could it mean King David, who was a descendant of Judah? Certainly, some local nations did come under his authority but not all the nations. Or could it mean one of David's direct descendants?

As the years went by, the Egyptians made the Israelites into slaves. They remained in Egypt for 400 years until God intervened and delivered them through Moses. They then spent 40 years travelling through the wilderness until eventually Joshua took them into the Promised Land. Joshua had originally been named by his parents in Egypt, 'Hoshea', which means 'Saviour'. Moses changed his name to 'Joshua' as he was not to be the Saviour, only the Lord can save. Joshua means just that, 'The Lord saves'. It is no coincidence that many years later Mary was told that her son was to be called 'Jesus', which was the Hebrew version of 'Joshua' and also means 'The Lord Saves.'

Before the Jews crossed the Jordan river into the land of the Canaanites, Joshua sent two spies to reconnoitre the walled city of Jericho. We are then told the strange story of a woman, named Rahab, who protected these spies. Surprisingly this story is given a whole chapter. Why was she so significant? We learn that Rahab subsequently married Salmon one of the senior officers in Joshua's army. So why is that important? The answer is that they had a son who was called Boaz, who became the grandfather of Jesse, who became the father of King David. All these people were direct ancestors of Jesus, the Messiah.

Ruth was a Moabite girl who married a Jewish man who had fled to Moab as a refugee because of a famine. A whole book is given to tell us about this virtuous young lady. Why was she so significant? The reason is that she became a wife of Boaz and it was their son, Obed, who became the father of Jesse. All these people were direct ancestors of the Messiah.

It is as if there was a mind behind all these people that were picked out in the Old Testament who knew where the Messiah would come from.

The King

King David gave us many inspired prophecies about the future Messiah in the Psalms. The Lord had told him that the Messiah would be one of his direct descendants.

Subsequent prophets repeatedly reminded people of the future Messiah's pedigree. Jesse was David's father.

"A shot will come up **from the stump of Jesse**; from his roots a Branch will bear fruit. **The Spirit of the Lord will rest on him – the Spirit of wisdom and understanding, the Spirit of knowledge and of the fear of the LORD – and he will delight in the fear of the LORD. He will strike the earth with the rod of his mouth; and with the breath of his lips he will slay the wicked. Righteousness will be his belt and faithfulness the sash round his waist.**" Isaiah 11:1–5

Who could this be referring to?

"The oppressor will come to an end, and destruction will cease; the aggressor will vanish from the land. **In love a throne will be established; in faithfulness a man will sit on it – one from the house of David.**" Isaiah 16:5

The strange thing is that after the Jews returned from captivity in Babylon no further descendant of King David ever became king. We are told this 'King' will be faithful and righteous. Who is it talking about? Jeremiah was clear,

"The days are coming," declares the LORD, "when I will raise up to David a righteous branch, a King who will rule wisely and do what is just and right in the land. In his days Judah will be saved and Israel will live in safety. This is the name by which he will be called: The LORD our righteousness." Jeremiah 23:5–6

This is startling. A man, who will be a direct descendant of King David, will be identified as being the Lord God, and he will somehow become our righteousness. Because of him people of all nations could be forgiven for their sin and considered righteous. Jeremiah repeats this prophecy later.

"**In those days and at that time I will make a righteous Branch sprout from David's line; he will do what is just and right in the land. This is the name by which he will be called; The LORD our righteousness.**" Jeremiah 33:15–16

Again, it is remarkable for a Jew to have written this. A human descendant of David would be called 'The LORD'– that is a man would be called Jehovah. This man will be both a king and Jehovah.

Many years after the reign of David, the prophet Ezekiel was one of the captives in Babylon. There the Lord told him,

"**My servant David will be king over them**, and they will all have one shepherd. They will follow my laws and be careful to keep my decrees. **My dwelling place will be with them; I will be their God, and they will be my people**. Then the nations will know that I the LORD make Israel holy, when my sanctuary is among them forever." Ezekiel 37:24–28

This prophecy makes the very same claim. A human king will become the 'good shepherd' of God's people. They will all want to live under his direction. This people will be 'made holy' by the king himself.

The Saviour

In our home, we regularly hold a five-week course, with suppers beforehand, where any people interested in learning more about the Christian faith can come to discuss the issues and evidence. One of these evenings deals with the evidence that the story about Jesus is true. I like to read the following account taken from what I simply say is an old book. The group are asked who this is about, who they think wrote it and when it was written. This is what is read,

"**He was hated and rejected by people**. He had much pain and suffering. People would not even look at him. He was hated, and we didn't even notice him. But he took our suffering on him and felt our pain for us. We saw his suffering and thought God was punishing him. **But he was wounded for the wrong we did; he was crushed for the evil we did**. The punishment, which made us well, was given to him, and we are healed because of his wounds.

We all have wandered away like sheep; each of us has gone his own way. But the Lord has put on him the punishment for all the evil we have done. He was beaten down and punished, but he didn't say a word. He was like a lamb being led to be killed. He was quiet, as a sheep is quiet while its wool is being cut; he never opened his mouth.

Men took him away roughly and unfairly. He died without children to continue his family. **He was put to death; he was punished for the sins of my people**. He was buried with wicked men, and he died with the rich. He had done nothing wrong, and he had never lied. But it was the Lord who decided to crush him and make him suffer. **The Lord made his life a penalty offering, but he will still see his descendants and live a long life**. He will complete the things the Lord wants him to do. **After his soul suffers many things, he will see life and be satisfied**."

There are very few who don't recognise that this is about Jesus. Most assume that it must have been written sometime in the first century AD, probably by one of the disciples. The reaction, when they are told that this was written by the prophet Isaiah around 750 BC, can be astounding. This prophecy, from Isaiah 53:3–11 (New Century Version), is remarkable. It tells of a person who is killed to bear the sins of other people, rather like the sacrificial offering of a lamb. The astounding feature is that this person will then rise from the dead, his job done.

Isaiah is clearly talking about Jesus, God's chosen king, God's Messiah.

John the Baptist introduced Jesus by saying,

"Look, the Lamb of God, who takes away the sin of the world." John 1:29

The problem is that we today, like Israel of old, have rejected our Saviour largely because we think we don't need one. Moses recited this in his final song to Israel, it is about a Saviour they would reject:

"Jeshurun (Israel) grew fat and kicked; **filled with food, he became heavy and sleek. He abandoned the god who made him and rejected the rock his Saviour**." Deuteronomy 32:15

David himself echoed the need he had for a Saviour in one of his songs,

"The LORD is my rock, my fortress and my deliverer; my God is my rock, in whom I take refuge, my shield and the horn of **my salvation**. He is my stronghold, my refuge and **my saviour**." 2 Samuel 22:2–3

Isaiah told people of every nation the essential message that God wants us all to know,

"The LORD has made a proclamation to the ends of the earth: 'Say to the daughter of Zion, **'See your Saviour comes**! See, his reward is with him, and his recompense accompanies him' They will be called the Holy People, the Redeemed of the LORD..." Isaiah 62:11–12

The Christian message centres on Jesus, the Messiah, and the promise that those committed to him, as their Saviour and their Lord, are secure. The evidence of faith is that we each become 'holy' or set apart for God, earnestly committed to living effectively for the Saviour who has won our forgiveness.

The Prophet

The Lord had earlier told Moses that 'a prophet' would be raised up from the Jewish nation:

"The LORD your God will raise up for you a prophet like me from among your brothers, you must listen to him. I will raise up for them a prophet like you from among their brothers. I will put my words in his mouth, and he will tell them everything I command him. If anyone does not listen to the words that the prophet speaks in my name, I myself will call him to account." Deuteronomy 18:15–19

Who was this very important individual to be? He was to come 'from among your brothers', he would be an Israelite so the Muslim claim that Muhammad is this prophet does not fit. From then on, the Jews were looking out for this great prophet of God. After Jesus had miraculously fed the five thousand, people were saying,

"Surely this is the prophet who is to come into the world." John 6:14

People reacted to Jesus in a variety of ways. On the last day of the Feast of Tabernacles, when he had been teaching in Jerusalem, Jesus made a public declaration about who he really was.

"If anyone is thirsty let him come to me and drink. Whoever believes in me, as the scripture has said, streams of living water will flow out from him." By this, he meant the Spirit, whom those who believed in him were later to receive. On hearing his words, some of the people said, '**Surely this man is the Prophet**." John 7:37–40

Peter gave a sermon, soon after Jesus' resurrection, to a crowd that had collected after a lame man was healed. He explained that Jesus was the fulfilment of this promise given to Moses and for this reason all must listen to him. (Acts 3:18–22)

The Messiah's Birth

When the wise men came from the East to worship the newly born Messiah, they naturally went to Herod's palace first. Herod the Great knew nothing of the birth of a future King so he asked his wise men for details. They knew the Old Testament Scriptures and were able to point to the prophecy which said where the baby would be born. Herod was told,

"But you, **Bethlehem** Ephraphah, though you are still small among the clans of Judah, **out of you will come for me one who will be ruler over Israel, whose origins are from old, from ancient times**." Micah 5:2

This prophecy was known to be Messianic by Jewish scholars. The baby Messiah is described as having 'origins from old, from ancient times.' How can a baby, even one so special, have origins from ancient times? Paul explains this,

"Who, being in very nature God, did not consider equality with God something to be grasped, but made himself nothing, taking the very nature of a servant, being made in human likeness." Philippians 2:6–7

Although Jesus was born in this small town of Bethlehem, that had only around 200 houses and 1000 occupants when Jesus was born, he was raised in the small town of Nazareth up in Galilee. This also was foretold in another famous Messianic prophecy that is read at Christmas time in many churches,

"In the past, he humbled the land of Zebulun and the land of Naphtali but **in the future he will honour Galilee** of the Gentiles, by the way of the sea, along the Jordan – The people walking in darkness have seen a great light; on those living in the land of the shadow of death a light has dawned. **For to us a child is born, to us a son is given, and the government will be on his shoulders. And he will be called Wonderful Counsellor, Mighty God, everlasting Father, Prince of Peace. Of the increase of his government there will be no end**. **He will reign on David's throne** and **over his kingdom**, establishing and upholding it with justice and righteousness **from that time on and forever**." Isaiah 9:1–7

This remarkable Messianic prophecy foretells that the Messiah will come from Galilee. He will be born a baby yet will be divine. The titles given to him are very descriptive. The same word for 'wonderful' which also means 'incomprehensible', was used earlier in the Bible when Manoah, Samson's father, asked the angel of the LORD what His name was. The LORD's angel responded,

"Why do you ask my name, seeing it is 'wonderful'?" Judges 13:18

In other words, "Why do you ask my name, since it is beyond your understanding?"

This king will be 'Mighty God', 'Everlasting Father', 'Prince of Peace' and he will rule eternally. Again it is important to realise that for a Jew to call a man God and say he would live forever is remarkable. Only Jesus would ever fit this description.

The Messiah's Death

We have already seen in Isaiah 53 that the Messiah will die and then rise again. There is one prophecy that gives details as to how he will die. David wrote a Psalm that Jesus quoted as he was dying on the cross. He cried out,

'My God, my God, why have you forsaken me?' Psalm 22:1

Just as David felt forsaken by God, so did the Messiah as he took our sin. That is why there was darkness for three hours. God can have nothing to do with sin so he turned his back on his Son. Darkness symbolises the absence of God.

Just before he died Jesus cried out,

"It is finished."

This can be the meaning of the last verse of this Psalm.

The centre of the Psalm describes the death of a lonely man.

"I am poured out like water, and all my bones are turned to wax; it has melted away within me. My strength is dried up like a potsherd, and my tongue sticks to the roof of my mouth; you lay me in the dust of death. Dogs have surrounded me; a band of evil men has encircled me, they have pierced my hands and my feet. I can count my bones; people stare and gloat over me. They divide my garments among them and cast lots for my clothing." Psalm 22:14–18

As far as we know, death by crucifixion was first practiced by the Phoenician people around 500BC. This Psalm was written by David around 1000BC. How did he know the graphic details about how the Messiah would die? How did he know that severe dehydration was a feature of such deaths. Furthermore, he describes how the executioners would split up the clothes of the condemned man but would cast lots for one article. John described the crucifixion of Jesus and noted the following,

"When the soldiers crucified Jesus, they took his clothes, dividing them into shares, one for each of them, with the undergarment remaining. 'Let's not tear it.' they said to one another, 'Let's decide by lot who will get it." John 19:23–24

The King Is Coming

The certain coming of God's king should change everything, certainly the way we live. Zechariah was a post-exilic prophet, living around 500BC.

"Shout and be glad, O Daughter of Zion. For I am coming, and I will live among you," declares the LORD. "**Many nations will be joined with the LORD in that day and become my people. I will live among you** and you will know that the LORD Almighty has sent me." Zechariah 2:10–11

Again it is the Lord God himself who will come and live in his world and people of every nation will become his people, they will join his kingdom. The same prophet describes one feature of the Messiah's life,

'Rejoice greatly, O Daughter of Zion! Shout, Daughter of Jerusalem. See, your king comes to you, righteous and having salvation, gentle and riding on a donkey, on a colt, the foal of a donkey.' Zechariah 9:9

By fulfilling this prophecy when Jesus rode into Jerusalem on a donkey on the first Palm Sunday (John 12:12–19) he was yet again claiming to be this Messiah of God.

The Son of Man

Jesus is referred to as the 'Son of Man' 88 times in the New Testament. It is the primary title Jesus used when referring to Himself (e.g., Matthew 12:32; 13:37; Luke 12:8; John 1:51).

At first, this seems strange as Jesus was at pains to point out that he was the one and only Son of God. Jewish people could not accept that a man could be God, even though God had appeared to Adam, Abraham and Jacob in human form. The probable reason Jesus used this phrase was to emphasise that he was fully human. This remarkable prophecy in Daniel that has been quoted earlier looks forwards to the day when a man will be accepted by God as his equal and who will then reign over God's kingdom for ever.

"In my vision at night, I looked, and there before me was one like **a son of man**, coming with the clouds of heaven. He approached the Ancient of Days and was led into his presence. **He was given authority, glory and sovereign power; all nations and peoples of every language worshiped him. His dominion is an everlasting dominion that will not pass away, and his kingdom is one that will never be destroyed.**' Daniel 7:13–14

Famously in 1779 Frederick the Great was discussing the existence of God with the Marquis D'Argens. The Emperor asked the Marquis,

'Can you give me one single irrefutable proof of God?'

'Yes, your Majesty, the Jews.'

There are over three hundred and thirty prophecies about the Messiah in the old Jewish Scriptures. This Messiah would be born into the Jewish tribe of Judah. He would be born in Bethlehem. He would live whilst the temple was still standing, as he would visit it. He would die by crucifixion (even though there is no evidence that crucifixion was practiced when King David described this) in Psalm 22. He would then overcome even death itself, rise from the dead and then rule God's kingdom forever. These prophecies are staggering.

Chapter 10
The Real Jesus

It appears that we all want heroes to follow, it may be a pop star, a sportsman or even a politician. There is something in our heroes we admire, even though we may disapprove about some aspects of their lives, particularly when their private lives are investigated. In contrast, Jesus stands out, he had a sincere integrity about him. It is no surprise that he developed such a following, thousands followed him around.

Jesus' Healing Ministry

The gospels describe how both his close followers and the masses were astounded by the miracles he performed. These were publicly performed and even non-Christian writers, such as Josephus refer to the miracles Jesus performed.

Jesus was a real person

Before asking whether Christianity is true, whether the resurrection happened, it is helpful to look at the unbiased facts concerning Jesus. He was a real person who lived and died in first century Palestine. This fact is supported by both neutral and hostile sources.

Suetonius wrote about the lives of Roman Emperors. He describes some rioting that took place in Rome in 49 AD, during the reign of Emperor Claudius. It seems that the Jews were angry about the Christians. He wrote,

'He expelled the Jews from Rome, on account of the riots in which they were constantly indulging, at the instigation of Chrestus.'

Jesus was not only a real person but his impact was being noticed as far away as Rome just sixteen years after his crucifixion.

Luke records in Acts that there were Christians in Italy very early on. St Paul landed in the town of Puteoli (modern-day Puzzuoli) in 61AD (Acts 28:13–14). This lies about thirty miles west of Pompeii which was destroyed in 79 AD.

Paul mentions that there were Christians in Puteoli, which means that followers of Jesus were already to be found in smaller towns around Naples.

Tacitus writes about the early followers of Jesus who Nero blamed for the Great Fire of Rome in 66AD, just 33 years after the crucifixion of Jesus. He wrote,

"The originator of that name, Christus, had been executed when Tiberius was Emperor by order of the procurator, Pontius Pilatus. But the deadly cult, they checked for a time, was now breaking out again not only in Judea the birthplace of this evil but even throughout Rome, where all the nasty and disgusting ideas from all over the world pouring and find a ready following."[57]

Josephus was a commander of the Jewish forces in the northern Judea, when the Jews revolted against Rome in AD66. He became an important historian and talks about Pontius Pilate, John the Baptist, Herod, Caiaphas the high priest, and James, the brother of Jesus, who became an early martyr. He said about Jesus,

"At that time, there was a wise man called Jesus, and his conduct was good and he was known to be virtuous. Many among the Jews in other nations became his disciples. Pilate condemned him to be crucified and to die, but those who had become his disciples did not abandon his discipleship. They reported that he appeared to them three days after his crucifixion and that he was alive. Accordingly, he was perhaps the Messiah concerning whom the prophets have reported wonders; and the tribe of Christians, so named after him, have not disappeared to this day."[58]

Pliny the Younger was sent to govern Bithynia, a small state in northern Turkey, around A.D. 112. He wrote many letters on a variety of subjects to his friend, the Emperor Trajan.

---

[57] Tacitus, Annals XV.44
[58] Antiquities XVIII.63

Jesus was crucified by the Romans

Jesus death was an accepted fact throughout the ancient world. The early church and secular historians confirmed this. A Jewish Rabbi, Samuel Sandmel, investigated their evidence and concluded,

"Certain bare facts are historically not to be doubted. Jesus, who emerged into public notice in Galilee when Herod Antipas was its Tetrarch, was a real person, the leader of a movement. He had followers, called disciples. The claim was made, either by him or for him, that he was the long-awaited Jewish Messiah. He journeyed from Galilee to Jerusalem, possibly on the 29th or 30, and there he was executed, crucified by the Romans as a political rebel. After his death, his disciples believed that he was resurrected, and had gone to heaven, but would return to earth at the appointed time for the final divine judgment of mankind.[59]"

The Munich Talmud manuscript of Sanhedrin 43a preserves passages censored out of printed editions, including the controversial trial of *Yeshu Notzeri* Jesus of Nazareth. This is the earliest full manuscript Talmud. Chronological analysis of the layers in this tradition suggests that the original words were:

"On the eve of Passover, they hung Jesus of Nazareth for sorcery and leading Israel astray."[60]

His dignified burial is also widely accepted. John A. T. Robinson a New Testament scholar argued that the burial of Jesus in a tomb is one of the earliest and best-attested facts about Jesus.[61]

The empty tomb is also felt to be a historical fact. Those who reject this tend to do so for theological and not historical reasons.[62]

---

[59] Rabbi Samuel Sandmel, A Jewish Understanding of the New Testament, 3rd ed. Woodstock, Vermont: Jewish Lights Publishing, 2010, 33)

[60] Marvin Heller, http://www.printingthetalmud.org/essays/7.pdf

[61] John A. T. Robinson, 'The Human Face of God' Philadelphia: Westminster Press, 1973 p. 131

[62] D. H. van Daalen, 'The Real Resurrection', London: HarperCollins, 1972, p. 41

The disciples met the risen Christ

They not only saw the risen Christ but ate meals and talked with him on several occasions. Once over five hundred people met the risen Christ on one occasion. They then went on to tell everybody they met of this fact. When on trial none of the disciples backed down from asserting this fact. Eleven out of the twelve disciples were killed for continuing to assert that Jesus was the divine Messiah and that he did rise from the dead as the old Jewish Scriptures foretold. Would they all die for a lie?

The Roman and Jewish authorities could not find Jesus' body after the resurrection. That they sought is strong evidence that the tomb had been found empty. The authorities would have destroyed the apostles' story if only they could have found his body or even arrested the risen Jesus.

The hostile sources that present a different rationale for the empty tomb could never present a body. While this does not necessarily prove the resurrection, it does leave the door open to other possible explanations. As Michael Horton concludes,

"Although unable to locate Jesus, dead or alive, the very fact that Jewish and Roman leaders sought alternative explanations for the resurrection demonstrates that the empty tomb was a historical fact. For the gospel story to have come to an easy and abrupt end, the authorities would only have had to produce a body."

The following historical facts which must be explained by any adequate historical hypothesis:

1. The extraordinary rapid expansion of the early church in spite of political opposition.

2. An early creed or kerygma of the church was recorded by Paul in 1 Corinthians 15: 3–8. Paul says he is repeating a tradition which he himself received.

'For I delivered to you as of first importance what I also received, that…'

This confirms that what follows was a very early creed as 1 Corinthians was written in 55AD, just twenty-two years after the resurrection. It centres on the death, burial and resurrection of Jesus, and then gives a list of witnesses to the resurrection. This primitive formula adds an addition by Paul of his experience of the risen Christ.

"Christ died for our sins according to the Scriptures,
that he was buried,

that he was raised on the third day according to the Scriptures,
and that he appeared to Cephas,
and then to the Twelve.

After that, he appeared to more than five hundred of the brothers and sisters at the same time, (most of whom are still living, though some have fallen asleep.)

Then he appeared to James, then to all the apostles, and last of all he appeared to me also, as to one abnormally born." 1 Corinthians 15:3–7

Paul then added,

"Last of all, as to one untimely born, he appeared also to me." 1 Corinthians 15:8

3. He surely added the phrase, 'most of whom are still living,' as further assurance that the resurrection really happened, as those people could still be interviewed and give their testimony.

Jesus' teaching

Jesus' teaching was so new. He taught that God looked at people's hearts and not their outward behaviour or social acceptability. He stresses the reality of God's final judgment at the end of our lives here on earth and of the reality of heaven and hell. He taught that any person, including the oppressed and poor can be admitted into God's kingdom. He taught as if he knew what he was talking about.

Most striking is the fact that Jesus taught so much about himself. When I was at school, a schoolmaster told our class that Jesus never claimed to be God. I don't think that that master could have read the New Testament. Jesus made some astonishing statements, claiming to be God's Messiah. Everyone knew that the Jewish Scriptures, our Old Testament, are all about God who alone could save people and give eternal life. When Jesus was summarising the evidence that supports his claim to have come directly from the Father, he said to the religious leaders, who thought they were authorities on Scripture,

"You diligently study the Scriptures because you think that by them you possess eternal life. These are the Scriptures that testify about me, yet you refuse to come to me to have life." John 5:39–40

After his resurrection, Jesus talked with two disciples as they walked to Emmaus,

"And beginning with Moses and all the Prophets, he explained to them what was said in the Scriptures concerning himself." Luke 24:27

Nothing could be clearer than the discussion Jesus had had with Jews when they asked him,

"Who do you think you are?"

Jesus replied, "Your father Abraham rejoiced at the thought of seeing my day; he saw it and was glad."

"You are not yet fifty years old." The Jews said to him, "And you have seen Abraham!"

"I tell you the truth," Jesus answered, 'before Abraham was born, **I am**!' At this they picked up stones to stone him' John 8:57–59

They wanted to stone him for blasphemy; Jesus had dared to use the divine name, 'I am', for himself.

Jesus claimed he had the right to forgive people their sin against God, which only God can do. Jesus said to a paralysed man,

"Son, your sins are forgiven."

This created uproar amongst the rabbis listening.

"Why does this fellow talk like that? He's blaspheming! Who can forgive sins but God alone?" Mark 2:5,7

On another occasion, some Jews gathered round Jesus in the temple and asked him directly, "How long will you keep us in suspense? If you are the Christ, tell us plainly."

Jesus answered, "I did tell you, but you do not believe. The miracles I do in my Father's name speak for me…I and the Father are one." Again the Jews picked up stones to stone him, but Jesus said to them,

"I have shown you many great miracles from the Father. For which of these do you stone me?"

"We are not stoning you for any of these," replied the Jews, "but for blasphemy, **because you, a mere man, claim to be God**." John 10:4–33

On one occasion, Philip, a disciple of Jesus, asked him,

"**Lord, show us the Father** and that will be enough for us." John 14:8

In answer to this question, Jesus said,

"Don't you know me Philip, even after I have been among you such a long time and yet you do not know me, Philip? Anyone **who has seen me has seen the Father**. How can you say, 'Show us the Father?' Don't you believe that I am in the Father and the Father is in me." John 14:9

At his trial before the Sanhedrin Caiaphas asked him outright,

"Are you the Christ, the Son of the Blessed One?"

"I am," said Jesus. "And you will see the Son of Man sitting at the right hand of the mighty one and coming on the clouds of heaven." Mark 14:61–62

The last part of Jesus reply is a reference to a well-recognised Old Testament Messianic passage which tells of a man being worshipped and ruling eternally as God,

"In my vision, I looked, and there before me was one like **a son of man, coming with the clouds of heaven**. He approached the Ancient of Days and was led into his presence. He was given authority, glory and sovereign power; all peoples, nations and men of every language **worshipped him**. His dominion is an everlasting dominion that will not pass away, and **his kingdom is one that will never be destroyed**." Daniel 7:13–14

This Jesus, who repeatedly made such outlandish claims, also healed the sick and even raised the dead. He repeatedly taught his disciples that he would be executed but would rise again after three days. This he proceeded to do!

C.S. Lewis, the writer of the Narnia stories, famously wrote,

"I am trying here to prevent anyone saying the really foolish thing that people often say about Him: **I'm ready to accept Jesus as a great moral teacher, but I don't accept his claim to be God. That is the one thing we must not say.** A man who was merely a man and said the sort of things Jesus said would not be a great moral teacher. He would either be a lunatic – on the level with the man who says he is a poached egg – or else he would be the Devil of Hell. You must make your choice. Either this man was, and is, the Son of God, or else a madman or something worse. You can shut him up for a fool, you can spit at him and kill him as a demon or you can fall at his feet and call him Lord and God, but let us not come with any patronising nonsense about his being a great human teacher. He has not left that open to us. He did not intend to. Now it seems to me obvious that He was neither a lunatic nor a fiend: and consequently, however, strange or terrifying or unlikely it may seem, I have to accept the view that He was and is God."[63]

It was the mass of evidence, accumulated from living closely with Jesus over three years, that convinced his disciples that Jesus was indeed the Son of God. Why else would they give their lives to tell the world that God had visited this

---

[63] Lewis, C. S., 'Mere Christianity', London: Collins, 1952, pp. 54–56.

planet as a person and had been crucified so that men's rebellion against God could be forgiven? The convincing evidence for his resurrection combined with the astounding, well documented growth of the early church is impossible to explain without Jesus' claims being true.

The evidence for the historical Jesus and his resurrection and the transforming effect he had on the world is overwhelming. One of the world's leading Jewish theologians, the late Pinchas Lapide, declared,

"I accept the resurrection of Jesus not as an invention of the community of disciples, but as an historical event."[64]

He was convinced by all the evidence that the God of Israel had raised Jesus from the dead.

Jesus' love

To be loved is essential if we are to become well balanced individuals. One of the primary characteristics of God is that he is a 'God of love' (1 John 4:8,16). Other gods, as the ancient Greeks and Romans knew, tend to be selfish, unkind, sadistic and immoral.

The Lord God met Moses on Mount Sinai and described who he is,

"And he passed in front of Moses, proclaiming, '**The Lord, the Lord, the compassionate and gracious God, slow to anger, abounding in love and faithfulness, maintaining love to thousands, and forgiving wickedness, rebellion and sin.** Yet he does not leave the guilty unpunished; he punishes the children and their children for the sin of the parents to the third and fourth generation." Exodus 34:6–7

Not surprisingly, this also perfectly describes the character of Jesus. He really cared for those in need and went out of his way to help others. He was willing to give up his life selflessly for others. Yet when some people stubbornly opposed him, he was not a mouse but a lion. When his Father's temple was being abused he was rightly livid. He had strong principles and this is the sort of leader that people respect.

Professor Tom Torrance was an eminent theologian in Edinburgh. As a young man during the second World War he was a chaplain's assistant in Italy,

---

[64] Pinchas E. Lapide, Wilhelm C. Linss (Translator), 'The Resurrection of Jesus: A Jewish Perspective'

as the Allied troops advanced. He met a young soldier who was mortally wounded. He knelt down beside him but before he could say a word the lad asked him,

"Chaplain, is God like Jesus?"

A remarkable question, to which the only answer is 'Yes.' This is what the chaplain shared with that soldier and it was subsequently his joy to pray with the lad, assuring him that God welcomes a penitent sinner, just as Jesus did.

Chapter 11
Did Jesus Rise from the Dead?

The resurrection is the cornerstone of the Christian faith – if it did not occur, then Christianity is in ruins. The apostle Paul recognised this when he wrote:

"For if Christ has not been raised, your faith is futile; you are still in your sins." 1 Corinthians 15:17

It is the final proof that Jesus is who he claimed to be. The resurrection was prophesied in the Old Testament, foretold by Jesus in the New and is the foundation of early church teaching. When Paul started to discuss the Christian claims on his visit to Athens, he kept talking about 'Jesus and Anastasis'. He was not talking about two gods, as some casual listeners supposed, but was telling them about 'Jesus and the resurrection', *anastasis* being Greek for 'resurrection'.

The resurrection is so central to the Christian faith that it is not surprising that several attempts have been made to explain the event away.

Was the wrong person executed?

This theory proposes that, if the wrong man was executed, it would be a simple matter for Jesus to appear fit and well and claim to have risen from the dead, and so convince his gullible disciples. It is significant that this was never proposed by the early opponents of the Christian faith. It is simply not tenable.

Jesus was very well-known. He had been publicly tried and executed. When on the cross, he had been seen by his mother and family, his disciples, Jewish opponents, and Roman authorities. No one had any doubt that the condemned man was Jesus, the preacher and miracle worker. When he was seen again alive on the third day, some disciples saw that he had wounds where nails had penetrated his wrists and feet, and another in his side where the spear had penetrated.

Could he have passed out on the cross?

The 'Today' newspaper of 27 April 1991 ran a startling feature on its front page, with the headline, 'JESUS DID NOT DIE ON CROSS.' It was proposed that Jesus was still alive when taken from the cross, and that placing him in a cool place would have revived him. This theory was first propounded at the end of the 18th century and has appeared every generation since. Let us look at some of the relevant facts.

1. *Jesus was first subjected to a Roman flogging.*

He was stripped of his clothes, and his wrists were tied to the top of the pole. The instrument used was a flagrum, which consisted of a handle with several leather thongs, each having jagged pieces of lead tied to the ends. The shoulders, back, buttocks and legs of Jesus were repeatedly flayed by this instrument until the centurion in charge decided that Jesus had had enough. It was not uncommon for muscle to be ripped and bone to be exposed. Unsurprisingly, people could die from a Roman flogging alone.

2. *The march*

The condemned man had to carry the heavy crossbar of his crucifix (the 'patibulum') through the city to the place of execution.

The execution party would often take a long route through the town to warn as many as possible of the consequences of rebellion against the authorities. A soldier would walk ahead of the condemned man with a notice proclaiming his crime.

It is not surprising that, after the flogging, Jesus was so weakened that he collapsed and an onlooker, Simon of Cyrene, was commandeered to carry it for him. These crossbars were often the long pieces of strong wood used to bar doors and could weigh nearly 112lbs. The place of crucifixion was not a 'green hill far away' but was almost certainly by the side of a main road leaving the northern side of Jerusalem. This would give the maximum deterrent effect.

3. *The execution*

At the execution site, the upright of the crucifix was laid on the ground and the crossbar tied to it firmly. Jesus was then held down on the cross and long nails were struck through each forearm, and then one nail was hit through the calcanea, the heel bones, holding the legs in a flexed position. The whole structure was then lifted up and dropped into a hole in the ground. His feet would only be about 18 inches off the ground. A small wooden seat, a 'sedile', was nailed to the upright to take some of the victim's weight. This also had the effect of prolonging the agony.

The victims suffered severe pain and cramps in their arms and legs, and breathing became very difficult. The victim cannot keep still. If he slumps, he cannot breathe in – and if he pushes up to breathe, he gets an excruciating pain from his feet. This exhausts, shocks and weakens him. The small seat helped in this regard but also prolonged the agony. The longest recorded time that anyone survived on a cross was nine days. Jesus was crucified at 9am and was dead by 3pm.

4. *The guards*

Each condemned man was guarded by four Roman soldiers. It was a capital offence for the soldiers to leave until death had occurred. If they wanted to bring on an early death, one of the soldiers would hit the lower legs with a mallet, and break the bones. This practice was called 'crurifragium'. The pain, blood loss and inability to push themselves up to help breathing rapidly brought on death. In the late afternoon on the day of Jesus' crucifixion, they did break the legs of the two thieves crucified either side of Jesus. They saw that Jesus was already dead, but, as a final check, they thrust a spear into his side. It is not possible that the soldiers could have left Jesus still alive.

5. *The body was asked for*

That evening, two of the Jewish political leaders, Joseph of Arimathea and Nicodemus, who were secret disciples of Jesus, went to Pilate and asked if they could have his corpse.

Pilate was surprised that Jesus had died so soon and he summoned the centurion in charge. Having the death confirmed, he gave permission for the body to be released for burial. It is inconceivable that the centurion got this wrong. He had too much to lose – it was a capital offence to make this kind of mistake.

6. *The burial*

The body was removed from the cross, and taken to a burial chamber. This new sepulchre belonged to Joseph of Arimathea, and both he and his friend, Nicodemus, washed Jesus' body according to Jewish customs, and dressed him in grave clothes. They obviously had no doubt that Jesus was dead as they then embalmed the body. The embalming substance consisted of pungent aromatic spices called 'aloes', made by pounding fragrant wood into dust, mixed with a sticky resin called 'myrrh'; 75 pounds of spices alone were used. This would have been enough to give a permanent general anaesthetic to the fittest man, let alone a corpse! The body was then wrapped in white linen up to the neck, with a separate head cloth to support the jaw. It was extremely difficult to remove this resin from the skin, yet, after his resurrection, no mention is made of the odour or stickiness that would normally still be present even after multiple baths!

7. *The closure of the tomb*

The opening of the tomb was closed with 'a very large stone'. One ancient manuscript of Mark's gospel adds, 'which 20 men could not roll away'. On the third morning, three women came to the tomb to add some more spices to Jesus' body, but recognised that three of them would have no chance of rolling back that stone. There is no way, therefore, that Jesus could have naturally done this, singlehandedly.

8. *The sealing of the tomb*

The tomb was formally sealed. This was done by stretching a cord across the stone, fixing both ends with clay which were stamped with the Roman Governor's insignia.

A Roman guard then protected the tomb. This guard was probably the standard guard of sixteen soldiers. Four of these would have been on duty at any time, but the others needed to be available for back-up. Matthew records that, after the resurrection, some of these guards reported to the chief priests what had happened. Presumably, they were looking for Jewish support, so that they would put in a good word with the Roman authorities, as the soldiers had failed in their responsibilities and faced serious penalties. After a high-level meeting of the Jewish leaders, they were given a large sum of money and were told to say that the disciples had come in the night and had stolen the body whilst they were asleep. It would have had to be a large bribe with other assurances for the soldiers to risk their reputations and lives! It is very difficult to conceive how the disciples could have outwitted an armed Roman guard in this way.

The breaking of a Roman seal was automatically investigated and those responsible would be punished by crucifixion upside down. It is significant that no action was taken in this case.

9. *The tomb was visited*

On the Sunday morning, Mary Magdalene went early to the tomb and found that the stone had been moved well away from the entrance of the tomb. She ran to tell Peter and John, who also came running. There in the tomb were the strips of grave clothes still lying in their place, with the head cloth next to them. As soon as John saw this, he believed that the resurrection had taken place. The position of the clothes, lying there as if the body had passed out of them, gave no other alternative. When John entered the tomb, we read, 'He saw and believed' (John 20:8).

10. *Jesus appeared to his followers*

When Jesus appeared to Mary Magdalene and, later that evening, to the other disciples, they had no doubt that Jesus had been resurrected. He was not in the dazed, ill state that he would be in if he had recovered from three days' unconsciousness. They studied his wounds – it was the same man.

On that first Sunday afternoon, Jesus joined two disciples, Clopas and his companion, possibly his wife, as they walked to their home in Emmaus. Emmaus was a village seven miles away from Jerusalem. Jesus talked with these two on the way there, discussing all the Old Testament prophecies about the Messiah. It was only when they entered their home and sat down for some food that they recognised who was with them. He obviously had no odour from the embalming resin on him. As a doctor, I find this story very striking. Have you ever tried to walk with a twisted ankle? I cannot see how Jesus could normally have walked even two yards after having a large Roman nail driven through both his ankles, let alone the 14 miles to Emmaus and back, and not hobble!

11. The blood and water

The final proof that Jesus must have died on the cross is one I find utterly convincing.

It comes from one sentence in John's record of the crucifixion:

'Instead one of the soldiers pierced Jesus' side with a spear, bringing a sudden flow of blood and water. The man who saw it has given testimony, and his testimony is true.' John 19:34–35

Out of the spear wound came a flow of first blood and then water. This must have collected in one of the body cavities of Jesus. We do know that the blood of animals and humans that are tortured to death does not clot (this is due to circulating anti-clotting chemicals called 'fibrinolysins'). When blood is left to stand, it separates into the red cells which drop to the bottom, leaving the clear plasma above. There seems to be no other reasonable explanation of what John saw, other than that the spear pierced a large cavity which had filled up with blood just before Jesus died and that this blood had separated into the red cells and plasma. It would take at least half an hour after death for this separation to occur. It could not have occurred if Jesus had fainted.

I am interested in which cavity the spear could have hit. The inside of the heart itself is too small to contain enough blood to produce this effect. The only other possibilities are the cavities around the lung (pleural cavity), and the cavity around the heart (pericardial cavity). Just before Jesus died, he 'cried out with a loud voice'. When people have a pleural cavity full of fluid, they are gasping for breath – so this does not fit. The only viable possibility is that, just before he died, there was a tear in his heart which led to a rapid filling of the pericardial space with blood. This itself would rapidly stop the heart due to what doctors call 'cardiac tamponade'. It is interesting that Jesus did die a 'cardiac type' death – he was not comatosed but awake when he realised something was going wrong, and said 'It is finished', and suddenly died. It therefore seems likely that Jesus literally died of a broken heart.

From all the information that we have, from several sources, there can be no doubt that Jesus did die on that cross and rise again.

The Disciples and Others Were Convinced

After his resurrection, Jesus appeared to many different people in different ways. He first appeared to a solitary woman, Mary Magdalene, whose testimony was not legally valid. Details such as this give the story authenticity. If the story was invented, a first appearance to a man would have made the story more emphatic and impressive. He then appeared to the two depressed disciples walking home to Emmaus, and they were convinced. His final appearance on that first Sunday was to the disciples meeting secretly behind locked doors; they were thrilled to see Jesus again. Only Thomas was missing, and, subsequently, he was sceptical about the other disciples' accounts and insisted that he could not accept the resurrection unless he saw Jesus and his wounds for himself. Thomas was present when Jesus joined them again the following Sunday, when Jesus said to him:

"Stop doubting and believe," Thomas said to him, "my Lord and my God."

Then Jesus told him, "Because you have seen me, you have believed; blessed are those who have not seen and yet have believed." John 20:27–29

After this, he appeared to over five hundred Christians at the same time. An early creed or kerygma of the church was recorded by Paul in 1Corinthians 15: 3–8. Paul says he is repeating a tradition which he himself received.

"For I delivered to you as of first importance what I also received, that."

This confirms that what follows was a very early creed as 1 Corinthians was written in 54AD, just 22 years after the resurrection. This creed was discussed on page 99.

One of the most telling pieces of evidence is what happened to these followers of Jesus after they had seen him. Prior to the death of Jesus, they had been weak and uncertain. They became utterly convinced, spending the rest of their lives telling the world about the facts as they saw them. Eleven out of the twelve apostles were probably martyred because of their convictions. Only John died naturally, and he had suffered as a prisoner on the island of Patmos. This behaviour is not explicable unless they were certain about Jesus. People may live a lie, but they will rarely die for a lie.

It was not only to his followers that Jesus appeared. Saul was an arch-enemy of the early Christians, and was directing their persecution on behalf of the Jewish leaders. He met the risen Jesus as he was travelling to Damascus. This meeting so convinced him that he spent the rest of his life, often at great personal risk, passing on the Christian message. He was finally beheaded just outside Rome.

James was the younger half-brother of Jesus who had mocked Jesus during his three-year teaching ministry. Who would be more difficult to convince than a younger brother? After the resurrection, Jesus appeared specifically to him (1 Corinthians 15:7). He was convinced, and eventually became the leader of the church in Jerusalem. James wrote an epistle in the New Testament, but was eventually stoned to death because of his convictions. Such men must have been certain to have persisted, with such determination and courage, against such odds.

At the first major sermon given by Peter, seven weeks after the death and resurrection of Jesus, Peter stressed these two facts saying: 'But God raised him from the dead' (Acts 2:24). Those listening must have known all about these events because, when they were challenged to make a decision as to who Jesus really was, about 3,000 people accepted the message and were publicly baptised as followers of Jesus the Messiah. Jewish people would not do such a thing lightly.

How else can the rapid growth of the early Christian church be explained? Those people must have been certain to have risked everything they had, including their lives, to tell others of God's intervention in the world.

Thomas Arnold was a Professor of History at Oxford, who specialised in Roman times. He was also a famous Headmaster of Rugby school. He said:

"I have been used for many years to studying the histories of other times, and to examining and weighing the evidence of those who have written about them, and I know of no one fact in the history of mankind which is proved by better and fuller evidence of every sort, to the understanding of a fair enquirer, than the great sign which God has given us that Christ died and rose again from the dead."
[65]

---

[65] McDowell J. 'Evidence that Demands a Verdict'. Campus Crusade, 1972:190–191 58

Lord Darling, a former deputy for the Lord Chief Justice of England between 1914–1918 and subsequently a Privy Councillor said:

"In favour of the resurrection as a living truth there exists such overwhelming evidence, positive and negative, factual and circumstantial, that no intelligent jury in the world could fail to bring in a verdict that the resurrection story is not true."[66]

Pinchas Lapide, a German Jewish Rabbi, also examined the evidence for the resurrection of Jesus he then concluded:

"I accept the resurrection of Easter Sunday not as an invention of the community of disciples, but as a historical event." [67]

---

[66] https://www.ministrytoday.org.uk/blog/2012/04/evidence-for-the-resurrection/

[67] Pinchas Lapide, 'The Resurrection of Jesus: A Jewish Perspective', SPCK, London 1984 p. 131

Chapter 12
The Jesus of History

Although Jesus was executed in his thirties in a backwater of the Roman Empire around 33 AD, he made so great a contemporary impact that much was written about him, both by his followers and by others who were not so sympathetic. The troubling statistic is that, in spite of all the evidence for the historic Jesus, 40% of adults in Britain and 46% of young people say they don't believe or aren't sure that Jesus was a real person![68] We will first look at some of the direct evidence for the historical Jesus by non-Christian writers.

Cornelius Tacitus

Tacitus wrote his Annals about AD 115. He describes how the early Christians had become such an embarrassment in Rome that the emperor Nero made them the scapegoats for the great fire of Rome that devastated the city in AD 64 – just over 30 years after the death of Jesus. It was widely felt that Nero had arranged for this fire but, in order to divert attention from himself, he blamed the Christians.

"But all human efforts, all the lavish gifts of the emperor, and the propitiations of the gods, did not banish the sinister belief that the conflagration was the result of an order (i.e. from Nero). **Consequently, to get rid of the report, Nero fastened the guilt and inflicted the most exquisite tortures on a class hated for their abominations, called Christians, by the populace. Christus, from whom the name had its origin, suffered the extreme penalty during the reign of Tiberius at the hands of one of our procurators, Pontius Pilatus,** and a most mischievous superstition, thus checked for the moment,

---

[68] https://talkingjesus.org/wp-content/uploads/2018/04/Talking-Jesus-dig-deeper.pdf

again broke out not only in Judæa, the first source of the evil, but even in Rome, where all things hideous and shameful from every part of the world find their centre and become popular. **Accordingly, an arrest was first made of all who pleaded guilty; then, upon their information, an immense multitude was convicted, not so much of the crime of firing the city, as of hatred against mankind."**[69]

Tacitus was obviously no friend of the Christians, but his evidence is therefore even more reliable. He confirms that Jesus lived in Judea and was executed by order of Pontius Pilate who was governor during the period AD 26–36. There were clearly large numbers of Christians in Rome just 34 years after the execution of Jesus and a contemporary historian is supporting the facts behind the Christian message even though he scorns it!

Pliny the Younger

Pliny was sent to govern Bithynia, a small state in northern Turkey, in about AD 112. He wrote letters on many subjects to the emperor Trajan. One of these concerned the problem he faced with the Christians in the area. He complained that, because of the new religion, people were deserting the pagan temples; that the sacred festivals were being discontinued for lack of popular support, and that the lucrative trade in animals for temple sacrifices was dwindling.

He therefore had the custom of arresting any Christians he could find and, if they persisted in their allegiance to Jesus, after being warned of the consequences, he had them executed. Pliny discovered that true Christians would rather die than pray to the pagan gods, or 'curse Christ' or make an offering to the emperor's statue. He described the habits of these early Christians:

"They were in the habit of meeting before dawn on a fixed day, they would recite, in turn, a hymn to Christ as God, and would bind themselves by oath to behave in a godly way. After the service, they would disperse but would meet later to eat together."

Pliny added that this 'perverse religious cult' was affecting 'large numbers of all classes'. Obviously, something very strong indeed was convincing these people to risk death by continuing their allegiance to Jesus.

---

[69] Tacitus, 'Annals' 15:44

Neither Pliny nor Trajan mention any crimes that Christians had committed, except for being followers of Jesus Christ and refusing to worship the Roman gods.

Pliny's practice was that if Christians refused to recant three times, they were executed. Pliny stated that his investigations had revealed nothing on the Christians' part but harmless practices and 'depraved, excessive superstition.' However, Pliny seems concerned about the rapid spread of this 'superstition'.

Pliny explains how the problems for the Christians in his area started.

"An anonymous document was published containing the names of many persons. Those who denied that they were or had been Christians, when they invoked the gods in words dictated by me, offered prayer with incense and wine to your image, which I had ordered to be brought for this purpose together with statues of the gods, and also cursed Christ – none of which those who are really Christians can, it is said, be forced to do – these I thought should be discharged. Others named by the informer declared that they were Christians, but then denied it, asserting that they had been but had ceased to be, some three years before, others many years, **some as much as twenty-five years**. They all worshipped your image and the statues of the gods, and cursed Christ. They asserted, however, that the sum and substance of their fault or error had been that they were accustomed to meet on a fixed day before dawn and sing responsively a hymn to **Christ as to a god**, and to bind themselves by oath, not to do some crime, but **not to commit fraud, theft, or adultery, not falsify their trust, nor to refuse to return a trust when called upon to do so**. When this was over, it was their custom to depart and to assemble again to partake of food – but ordinary and innocent food."

If some claimed they had been Christians twenty-five years before, that would bring us back to 87AD. The beliefs of this early church were clearly the same as those of the apostles. They believed that Jesus was God and recognised that to become a Christian meant a commitment to be holy, set apart for him.

Josephus

Josephus was a commander of the Jewish forces in the north of Judea when the Jews revolted against Rome in AD 66. He wrote two important histories. The Antiquities gave a history of the Jews up to AD 66 and the 'The Jewish War' gives a detailed account of the rebellion between AD 66 and 73. He was able to do this as, realising the eventual outcome, he had changed sides and became advisor on Jewish affairs to the Roman generals. He talks about many historical figures, including Pontius Pilate, John the Baptist, Herod, Caiaphas the High Priest, and James the brother of Jesus who became an early martyr when leading the church in Jerusalem. He wrote:

"At that time, there was a wise man called Jesus, and his conduct was good and he was known to be virtuous. Many among the Jews and the other nations became his disciples. Pilate condemned him to be crucified and to die, but those who had become his disciples did not abandon his discipleship. They reported that he appeared to them three days after his crucifixion and that he was alive. Accordingly he was perhaps the Messiah concerning whom the prophets have reported wonders; and the tribe of Christians, so named after him, have not disappeared to this day." Antiquities 23: 63

Elsewhere, Josephus acknowledged that Jesus was 'a doer of marvellous works'; in other words, a miracle worker. He also mentions the stoning of James, the brother of Jesus, who led the early church in Jerusalem:

"Ananias…convened the judges of the Sanhedrin and brought before them a man named James, the brother of Jesus who was called the Christ, and certain others. He accused them of having transgressed the law and delivered them up to be stoned." Antiquities 20:9

Suetonius

Suetonius wrote about the lives of the Roman Emperors. He describes some rioting that took place amongst the Jews in Rome in AD 49, during the reign of Emperor Claudius. The emperor reacted by banishing all Jews from the city:

"He expelled the Jews from Rome, on account of the riots in which they were constantly indulging, at the instigation of Chrestus." [70]

Luke refers to this expulsion in the Book of Acts. When Paul came to Corinth he met up with Aquila and his wife, Priscilla, who had recently arrived from Italy, 'because Claudius had ordered all the Jews to leave Rome' (Acts 18:2). It is apparent, therefore, that the message of Christ (or Chrestus) was already making a great impact in the capital of the empire just 17 years after the crucifixion of Jesus.

---

[70] Catharine Edwards. 'Lives of the Caesars, Suetonius', 2001 pp. 184, 203

All this evidence helps confirm the reliability of the records we have of the apostles, that are collected together in our New Testament.

Early Christian Writings

The Jewish copyists of the Old Testament scriptures were known to be meticulous in ensuring that exact copies of the scriptures were always made and that not even one letter in a word was misplaced. This same attitude was clearly held by the copyists of the apostolic writings as so many of the early manuscripts are virtually the same.

The early Christians frequently quoted the apostolic writings, and this is a further check that the New Testament, as we have it, is the same as it was when originally written.

Clement of Rome was one of the early leaders of the church in Rome, who died around AD 100. He wrote an open letter to the church at Corinth, known as 'I Clement', which is probably the earliest writing we have following the apostolic era. There are numerous quotes from both the Old Testament and New Testament books, demonstrating that, even at this early stage, the apostles' writings were considered authoritative as well as being the same as we have today.

Justin Martyr was a pagan who became a Christian at the beginning of the second century when an elderly stranger discussed with him the significance of the Jewish prophets who looked forward to Christ. Justin had already noted the extraordinary way the early Christians behaved when persecuted and he subsequently responded by committing his life to Jesus Christ, his maker. He soon began to teach others about Jesus, stressing that all should follow him because of the evidence that it was true. In his books, he quotes passages from the New Testament 330 times. He was martyred in Rome about AD 165.

Quadratus was an early Christian writer in Athens who presented a defence of the Christian faith to the Roman Emperor Hadrian when he visited Athens around 120 AD. He stressed the miracles of Jesus:

"The works of our Saviour were always present, namely those who were healed, those who rose from the dead. They were not only seen in the act of being healed or raised, but they remained always present, and not merely when the Saviour was on earth, but after his departure as well. They lived on for a considerable time, so much so that some of them have survived even to our own day."

The historian of the early church, Eusebius, tells us why Quadratus wrote this:

"…because certain wicked men had attempted to trouble the Christians. The work is still in the hands of a great many of the brethren, as also in our own, and furnishes clear proofs of the man's understanding and of his apostolic orthodoxy."

Eusebius also tells us of another early apologist,

"Aristides also, a believer earnestly devoted to our religion, left, like Quadratus, an apology for the faith, addressed to Adrian. His work, too, has been preserved even to the present day by a great many persons."[71]

It is significant that the early Christians went out of their way to stress, as being true, the most improbable aspect of Jesus' life – his miracles. It is significant that there is no mention of these miracles continuing to happen in his day. Normally people would play down anything that others will find difficult, in order to gain support.

Justin Martyr also wrote about the evidence supporting the Christian position in AD 150. He casually states: "That he performed these miracles you may easily satisfy yourself from the 'Acts of Pontius Pilate'."

Obviously, in Pilate's report, stored in the imperial archives in Rome, there was confirmatory evidence about the power of Jesus.

Irenaeus studied as a young man under Polycarp, who had been a disciple of John the apostle. He became bishop of Lyons in Gaul in AD 177 and wrote to counteract false teaching in the churches of his area, and to show that the Christian beliefs are predicted in the Old Testament. He quotes the books of the New Testament 1,819 times. He also gave some interesting insight into the background of the four gospel records:

"Matthew published his gospel among the Hebrews in their own tongue, when Peter and Paul were preaching the gospel in Rome and founding the church there. After their departure (or death), Mark, the disciple of and interpreter of Peter, himself handed down to us in writing the substance of Peter's preaching. Luke, the follower of Paul, set down in a book the gospel preached by his teacher.

---

[71] Eusebius, Hist. Eccl. IV.3.

Then John, the disciple of the Lord, who also leaned on his breast, himself produced his gospel, while he was living at Ephesus in Asia." [72]

Irenaeus also commented on the reliability of these records: "So firm is the ground upon which these Gospels rest that the very heretics themselves bear witness to them."

Archaeological Evidence

For the last 1,500 years, there has been an enormous increase in archaeological studies of the Bible countries and times. These have not only increased our knowledge of the background to the Bible stories but have also given great support to the Bible's claim to be the 'Word of God' and utterly reliable.

Sir William Ramsay, a Professor at Aberdeen University, was one of the most distinguished scholars. In his training, he had been led to believe that the Biblical stories were, to a considerable extent, mythical and were written many years after the events took place by unknown imaginative writers. Consequently, when he began his archaeological studies in Turkey, he had no confidence in the historicity of the New Testament records. However, he gradually began to realise that Luke, who wrote both the gospel and the Acts of the Apostles, was always right when new information became available. He finally concluded:

"Luke is a historian of the first rank; not merely are his statements of fact trustworthy, he is possessed of the true historical sense…in short, this author should be placed along the very greatest of historians." [73]

Let us look at one example. In Acts 13:7, Luke describes Sergius Paulus as 'proconsul' of Cyprus. Sir William Ramsay described, in 1912, a recently found stone which had the following inscription engraved on it in Latin:

"To L[ucius] Sergius Paullus the younger, Son of Lucius, one of four commissioners in charge of the Roman streets, tribune of the soldiers of the sixth legion." [74]

---

[72] Irenaeus, Adversus Haereses, 3.3.4.

[73] Sir William M. Ramsey, The Bearing of Recent Discovery on the Trustworthiness of the New Testament, Hodder & Stoughton, 1915.

[74] https://biblearchaeologyreport.com/2019/11/15/sergius-paulus-an-archaeological-biography/

This supports the presence of such a man, but he is not a proconsul and his name is spelt with a double 'l'. Later, however, Luke's reliability was confirmed when an old coin was found in Cyprus bearing the inscription: 'In the proconsulship of Paulus.' Note that only one 'l' was used here!

In 79 AD, Mount Vesuvius erupted and buried both Pompeii and Herculanum under volcanic ash. Bruce W. Longenecker has shown that there were undoubtedly Christians living in the fated town by that date, just 46 years after the death of Jesus.[75] Eighteen Christian crosses have been found carved into Pompeian Street paving stones. These crosses, laid out according to plan, seem to have acted as pointers leading to a bakery in the Insula Arriana Pollians. Here a cross was found, in a prominent place on the wall, made out of raised plaster. This appears to have been an early house church. In 61 AD, during a visit to the nearby harbour town in Puteoli, the Apostle Paul also mentioned the presence of a Christian community there, thirty miles west of Pompeii.

"From there, we set sail and arrived at Rhegium. The next day the south wind came up, and on the following day, we reached Puteoli. There we found some brothers and sisters who invited us to spend a week with them. And so we came to Rome." Acts 28:13–14.

There is other evidence that Christianity existed in Pompeii. The 'Christianos Graffito' was found in a large residence and reads, 'Audi Christianos…' ('Listen to the Christians'), and hints at the practice of preaching which helped the quick spread of the faith in the Roman world. The 'Vivit Cross' is a graffito in which the final 'it' has been made in the form of a cross. 'Vivit' is Latin meaning means, 'he lives' and this summarises a key teaching of the church – Jesus lives. The 'Meges stamp-ring' has a cross surmounting a symbol for eternal life. Such archaeological evidence strongly supports the evidence of early writers that the church grew very rapidly in the first century AD.

So much has been written on the reliability of the Biblical records. Again and again, the Bible has been proved to be the most reliable source book about ancient times. An eminent Jewish archaeologist, Nelson Glueck, has said, "It may be stated categorically that no archaeological discovery has ever controverted a biblical reference."

---

[75] Bruce W. Longenecker, 'The Crosses of Pompeii. Jesus-Devotion in a Vesuvian Town' Fortress Press 2016

There is also no ancient book for which there is anything like the same evidence to confirm that what we now hold is the same as was originally given. Over 20,000 ancient manuscripts containing all or part of the New Testament documents have been discovered so far. In contrast, we have only two manuscripts of the writings of Tacitus and seven of the writings of Pliny the Younger. Even Homer's Iliad has only 643 manuscripts.

In spite of all these manuscripts, the differences in the texts are few. Over 99.5 per cent of the text of the New Testament has no alternative wording. Sir Frederic Kenyon, who was director of the British Museum, wrote in his book *Our Bible and the Ancient Manuscripts*: "No fundamental doctrine of the Christian faith rests on a disputed reading."

The dating of these manuscripts is also important. Pliny first published his History in AD 77 but the earliest manuscript is about AD 850. Tacitus wrote his Annals in about AD 100, yet the earliest manuscript is AD 950. Of the ten manuscripts we have for Caesar's Gallic Wars, the earliest is around AD 850. The earliest New Testament document is probably the John Rylands Fragment, which is a small piece of papyrus containing five verses from chapter 18 of John's gospel, It was probably copied around AD 125. The Chester Beatty Papyri, contain most of the New Testament, and the Bodmer Papyri, containing a copy of John's gospel and most of Luke's gospel were both written about AD 200. The Codex Vaticanus contains papyri with most of the Bible, written about AD 350. The Codex Sinaiticus was also written in the mid fourth century and contains virtually all the New Testament and the majority of the Old. In all there are over 5,000 Greek manuscripts, and over 10,000 Latin manuscripts of parts of the New Testament, besides over 36,000 quotes from the New Testament in the writings of the early church fathers. It is on such extensive evidence that we can be confident that the New Testament we have is the same as was originally written.[76][77][78] Sir Frederick Kenyon also said,

"It cannot be too strongly asserted that in substance the text of the Bible is certain. The number of manuscripts of the New Testament, of early translations of it, of quotations from it, is so large that it is practically certain that the true

---

[76] Barnett P. 'Is the New Testament History?' London: Hodder and Stoughton, 1986:17

[77] France RT. Evidence for Jesus. London: Hodder and Stoughton, 1986:21

[78] Dowley T (ed). 'The History of Christianity'. London: Lion Publishing, 1977

reading of every doubtful passage is preserved in some one or other of the ancient authorities. This can be said of no other ancient book in the world."[79]

The great Bible scholar, Professor F.F. Bruce (1910–1990) was the Rylands Professor of Biblical Criticism and Exegesis at the University of Manchester. He declared:

"The variant readings about which any doubt remains among textual critics of the New Testament affect no material question of historic fact or of Christian faith and practice."[80]

Names and Grammar in the Gospels[81]

If the gospels are authentic first century writings, then textual criticism can support or disprove this. A person writing in a later time period or from a different geographical area would inevitably get place names and other details wrong. Yet latest scholarship has supported that the wording used is contemporary with both local geographical knowledge and word usage of the time. Historian David Hackett Fischer dubs this 'the rule of immediacy' and terms it 'the best relevant evidence.'[82]

Individual names also vary between different countries and times. Some fascinating research has compared the names that occur commonly in the New Testament with those of Jews living in Israel and surrounding countries at different times. In the New Testament, the two most common names are Simon and Joseph, 18.2 per cent of men mentioned in Acts and the Gospels having these names. In first-century Israel, the figure is very similar, 15.6 per cent having those names. Further analysis of other names shows a remarkable coherence between the other New Testament names of both men and women and first century Israel. These differ markedly from the names of Jews living in Egypt during the first century.

---

[79] Kenyon, Sir Frederic, 'Our Bible and the Ancient Manuscripts' London: Eyre and Spottiswoode, 1895 p. 10–11

[80] Bruce, F.F., The New Testament Documents: Are They Reliable? Grand Rapids, MI: Eerdmans, 1975, p. 19–20

[81] Peter Williams, https://www.youtube.com/watch?v=zTtdBpMMAFM

[82] David Hackett Fischer, "Historian's Fallacies: Toward a Logic of Historical Thought" (New York: Harper and Row, 1970), 62.

When this comparison of names is made between the names used in the New Testament, and the apocryphal gospels, which are dated later, there is much less similarity. This gives further internal evidence that the gospels were indeed accurate first century writings.

Another strong argument of textual critics is the vocabulary, spelling and grammar used. The textual critic G. D. Kilpatrick has noted that,

"No one has so far shown that the New Testament is contaminated with the grammar or orthography (spelling) of a later period."[83]

The Early Spread of Christianity

In 1945, an undisturbed tomb was found near Jerusalem. Inside were the bones of five people. The tomb had been sealed in AD 50, a coin of that date having been left inside. On one of the caskets were written the words, 'Jesus, help,' and on another was the inscription, 'Jesus, let him arise.' Though there is dispute in interpretation, this find not only confirms the early spread of the Christian faith, Jesus having been crucified around AD 30, but also confirms that they recognised who Jesus was – the man who is God who holds the keys to eternal destiny.

The Christian faith spread rapidly in those early years, not by armed force as Islam did, but against great opposition. These early Christians were liable to lose their jobs and even their lives if they were followers of Jesus, yet those becoming Christians increased rapidly. What was it that convinced so many?

The major argument used by the apostles and others as to why all should become Christians was that the message about Jesus was true. Jesus had clearly stated who he was and what he had come to do. His remarkable character supported his claim, but it was the miracles, and especially the resurrection, that so many people had seen, that really proved it. Furthermore, Jesus exactly fitted man's deepest needs for a purpose, forgiveness and a deep-seated desire for righteousness.

It is not a blind faith that they (and we) are asked to hold, but a faith based on irrefutable facts. Any honest person who rejects Jesus will have to find an explanation for all the various lines of evidence in support of his claim.

---

[83] John W. Wenham, "Christ and the Bible" (Downers Grove, Ill.: InterVarsity Press, 1973), 178–183.

Changed Lives Today

One of the main reasons that I was inclined to investigate the claims of Jesus was because of what I saw in some Christians' lives. They did seem to have a friendliness, openness and integrity that was attractive.

Charles Bradlaugh was a Victorian atheist who opposed Christianity. One day, he challenged a Christian minister to hold a debate, comparing the claims of Christianity with those of atheism. The minister, Hugh Price Hughes, agreed to the challenge on one condition – that Mr Bradlaugh bring with him a hundred people whose lives had been changed for the better by their commitment to atheism. If he did so, Mr Hughes would also bring along a hundred people whose lives had changed through knowing Jesus. Knowing that Mr Bradlaugh could not fulfil this demand, he offered to drop the number to first 50, then 20, then ten and finally one! Understandably, Mr Bradlaugh had to withdraw his invitation. He could not produce one man or woman in whom his beliefs had brought about a real change of character for the better. Atheism has no moral power to change lives, whereas Jesus is continually doing this. [84]

---

[84] https://emailmeditations.wordpress.com/2017/05/26/1506-challenge-accepted/

Chapter 13
Early Church Growth

This has fascinated many people. In spite of much official opposition and persecution the church grew extremely rapidly. The expulsion of Jews from Rome because of riots 'at the instigation of Chrestus,' the findings of Christian symbols and crosses in Pompeii, that was destroyed in 79AD, and the evidence of Pliny the Younger all support the Biblical evidence that many throughout the Roman world accepted their need for Christ. Rodney Stark, a sociologist of religion who has written extensively on the topic, asked:

"How did a tiny and obscure messianic movement from the edge of the Roman Empire dislodge classical paganism and become the dominant faith of Western civilisation?"

He attributes it to four factors,[85]

1. Friendships. Everyday friendships and the personal interactions of ordinary believers with outsiders are what makes the greatest difference. The early Christians were committed to personal evangelism.

2. Practical care. What distinguished Christians was their response to the all-too-frequent calamities of epidemics and natural disasters. Instead of fleeing to the countryside to escape the most recent plague, they stayed to care for their own – and for others. They knew that God loved them and that their own lives were in his hands, whether on earth or with him in heaven.

3. Their stance against immorality. Adultery, promiscuity, abortion, and infanticide were rife in the Roman world. The Christians' strong stance attracted others whose natural instincts were being appealed to.

---

[85] https://myocn.net/four-reasons-why-early-christian-church-grew-so-quickly/

4. Their real love. They knew that God loves his world and that he desires those who love him to also love their fellow man. This love will include addressing others' practical concerns as well as helping them spiritually.

Although these four factors are undoubtedly significant, it is difficult to see how they could have caused such an immediate response to the Christian message. There must be more. I suspect they overlook what Jesus and his apostles emphasised, that everybody needs to be forgiven their sin if they are to be acceptable to God. Everybody recognises that we are not what we should be and that we need God's forgiveness. Animal sacrifices, previously used to try and atone for sin, were obviously just a symbol for something greater. The death of a lamb cannot forgive my sin! When they heard about who Jesus was and what he had achieved on the cross, Jesus became very attractive. Here was 'the Lamb of God who takes away the sin of the world' (John 1:29), who could take away the sin from each person.

Another feature was the enthusiasm for Jesus that the early Christians demonstrated; such enthusiasm is very attractive.

Furthermore, there is the joy that Christians experience. C.S. Lewis called his autobiography, 'Surprised by Joy' as this was a major experience when he turned to God as a twenty-eight-year-old university don. What a shame it is when Christians do not have this experience of joy and peace. Joy and enthusiasm are certainly attractive and draw others to Saviour. The organist of Harrow parish church was Dr F.W. Farmer. The local Salvation Army had been invited to hold a joint service with them. Dr Farmer was upset by the enthusiastic way their drummer was hitting his drum and he asked him to hit the drum in a more delicate way. The drummer replied,

"Lord bless you, sir! Ever since I've been converted, I'm so happy I could bust the blooming drum."

This is the work of God in the Christian's life but, in addition, there is the factor of the work of the Holy Spirit himself in preparing other people to hear the gospel receptively. When God's Spirit prepares people by showing them their need, they will be drawn to Jesus when told about him.

As you read Christian biographies, a common theme is that people feel drawn to God. In Richard Wurmbrand's biography, 'In God's Underground,' he writes,

"I was like the man in the ancient Chinese story, trudging exhausted under the sun, who came to a great oak and rested in its shade. 'What a happy chance I found you,' he said.

But the oak replied, 'It is no chance. I have been waiting for you for 400 years.' Christ had waited all my life for me. Now we met."[86]

What happened to Richard Wurmbrand, a young Jew was striking. An elderly Jewish carpenter, living high up in a Rumanian Mountain village, was praying that God would allow him to lead one more Jew to Christ. The problem was that hardly any Jews ever visited his village. The Jewish born Richard Wurmbrand said, "Something irresistible drew me to that village."[87]

Those early Christians prayed that their message would be well received. No wonder Paul could write to the early churches, emphasising the need for prayer as they share the gospel, backed by a wise, graceful urgency.

"Devote yourselves to prayer, being watchful and thankful. And pray for us, too, that God may open a door for our message, so that we may proclaim the mystery of Christ, for which I am in chains. Pray that I may proclaim it clearly, as I should."

"Be wise in the way you act toward outsiders; make the most of every opportunity. Let your conversation be always full of grace, seasoned with salt, so that you may know how to answer everyone." Colossians 4:2–6

These early Christians needed to learn to 'devote themselves to prayer', to make this a major priority in order that God would open doors. Could this be why so many people do not find any doors opening today? They were also taught that they must relate well to outsiders. How can people see and hear the gospel if God's people are not active in making such relationships? God's people had to be graceful but certainly not a walk-over. They were to be the salt of society, standing firmly for God's truths and standards, even when they are unpopular.

When these truths are blunted, the church no longer has an incisive effect. This is well illustrated by the early history of the church in China.[88] In 1685, evidence was discovered at Sianfu, North-West China that a church existed there in the seventh and eighth centuries. A stone was found, known as the Sianfu Stone which shows that the Christian influence lasted nearly a century and a half. A Syrian missionary, named Olopan arrived in 635 AD and as a result of his work a church grew and lasted until 781 AD, the year when the stone was erected. It is clear from the stone that the Christians adjusted their teaching in order to

---

[86] Richard Wurmbrand, 'In God's Underground', W.H. Allen
[87] Told by Ian Barclay in 'The Facts of the Matter', Falcon 1977 p.34
[88] Recounted by Ian Barclay in 'The Facts of the Matter', Falcon 1977 p. 51

accommodate the wishes of Tihtsung, who occupied the Peacock throne, and his intelligentsia. The effect was catastrophic. In their attempts to win the local Buddhists and Confucians, who were opposed to the teachings about the death and resurrection of Jesus, they toned down this part of the story. The cross of Christ was 'vaguely kept in mind'. Real love will share with people the truths about Jesus, his sacrificial death to pay for our sin and his resurrection to prove his claim to be the very Son of God.

Another factor is that they worked together as a team. Ineffective churches are fragmented. John Wesley said, "God knows nothing of a solitary religion."

Christianity undoubtedly starts as a personal relationship with Jesus but it must never stay as a private relationship. Christians are called by God to become members of his kingdom so that we can work together for him. The church's motto could be,

"Divided we fall, together we stand."

The early church was unashamed to teach these doctrines, even if there was a high price for people to pay.

It is very hard to explain the extraordinary rapid expansion of the early church without it being a remarkable work of God. It appears to be just as supernatural as the freeing of the Children of Israel from captivity in Egypt, which was also highly improbable.

Chapter 14
Instincts and Innate Values

This for me has become a very powerful argument. After I had given a lecture in the University of Hertfordshire on the relationship between science and the Christian faith, I was surrounded by a group who were associated with 'The Atheist Society'. They tried to counter several of the arguments I had used for the need of a designer and creator by bringing up the theoretical possibility of there possibly being an infinite number of universes. I explained that even they would need a creator but we then moved on to the question of 'moral instincts'. They acknowledged that they also had 'gut feelings' that these values were valid. They thought that their lives did have a purpose. They instinctively believed that 'right and wrong', 'integrity' and 'honesty' mattered. They valued 'beauty', 'courage' and 'altruism' even though they could not explain where these ideals had come from.

All people have these human ideals even if they consider their origin and validity uncertain. 'The Who' made a record called 'The Seeker', which included the line,

"I've got values, but I don't know how or why."

Although values such as 'Goodness', 'Beauty', 'Truth', 'Honesty' and 'Courage' cannot be proved to the mechanistic scientist, they are nonetheless essential ingredients of human life. Indeed, these are the main features that distinguish humanity from other members of the animal kingdom. As these values diminish in a civilisation, so that civilisation is weakened. Human society and friendships rely on these virtues.

Everyone I have met believes in right and wrong, particularly when someone has done something against their own interests! Honesty and integrity are valued by all people. We all believe truth is important in our relationships. Our law courts are based on the search for truth and modern medicine relies on making a true diagnosis of the symptoms so that treatment that has been proved to be effective in similar cases can be given. Selfless love for others is universally applauded, whereas unkindness and cruelty are deplored. The question must be asked where these instincts come from. They are as innate as the ability of a baby to swallow its mother's milk or to cry when it is in some need. The Bible says that mankind has been made in the image of God. Could these moral instincts be one aspect of this?

How we hate it when someone hurts us by stealing our belongings or reputation by malicious gossip. We all feel they are wrong to do this – it is obnoxious behaviour. Yet we have all done what we know is wrong. We know that God has put in us the difference between 'Good and Evil' and that these values cannot be arbitrarily redefined however much some leaders may want to do so. Communist and Nazi leaders have tried to alter such values artificially – and have invariably come eventually to a downfall.

Jean-Paul Sartre was an existentialist writer who rejected the idea of God and any real meaning in life. However, he did have an innate moral sense. When he spoke out against the atrocities occurring in France during the Nazi occupation, which he considered to be immoral, his inner conflict came to the fore. His philosophy denied the presence of meaning, morality and purpose but his heart shouted out that there really is a right and wrong. He never wrote anything of substance after this.

The famous English poet, W. H. Auden moved to live in New York in 1939, when the Second World War began. The war and the Nazi atrocities led him to think through the greater issues in life. The Nazis had rejected orthodox morality. They made no pretence to uphold values such as honesty and justice in spite of the occasional religious comments by Hitler and other leaders to give the appearance of normality. They ridiculed love, a basic principle of Christianity, as being a sign of weakness. They taught,

"…to love one's neighbour as oneself was a command fit only for effeminate weaklings."[89]

Germany, being one of the most educated countries of the world, were now denying so much of what the west had long regarded as decent, honourable and true. W.H. Auden came to realise that nobody could assume that traditional

---

[89] W.H. Auden 'Modern Canterbury Pilgrims' ed. James A Pike (New York: A.R. Mowbray, 1956 p. 41 cited by Tim Keller in 'Encounters with Jesus' Hodder and Stoughton 2013 p. 13–14

values of freedom, reason, democracy and human dignity were self-evident. He wrote,

"If I am convinced that the highly educated Nazis are wrong, and that we highly educated English are right, what is it that validates our values and invalidates theirs? The English individuals who now cry to heaven against the evil incarnated in Hitler have no heaven to cry to. The whole trend of liberal thought has been to undermine faith in the absolute. It has tried to make reason the judge. But since life is a changing process, the attempt to find human space for keeping a promise leads to the inevitable conclusion that I can break it whenever I feel it convenient. Either we serve the Unconditional, or some Hitlerian monster will supply an iron convention to do evil by."[1]

When W.H. Auden was young, he had drifted away from the Christian faith but later he recognised that to make sense of life, a real God is needed and that he has to be part of our world. This led him back to reconsider the place of Jesus Christ. He came to recognise that Jesus was indeed God incarnate. This change came about when he recognised that there was an absolute quality in the traditional values that held society together – they were God's values that came from his character.

There is something in our nature that demands rational integrity. The origin of this desire for intellectual integrity that includes all areas of knowledge is another problem that is hard to solve without invoking a rational God who has created us in his own rational image.

There was a debate between the atheist, Bertrand Russell and the philosopher, Frederick Copleston. During the debate Mr Copleston asked,

"Mr Russell, you do believe in good and bad, don't you?"

Mr Russell replied, "Yes, I do."

"How do you differentiate between them?" challenged Mr Copleston.

"The same way I differentiate between yellow and blue," replied Mr Russell.

"But Mr Russell, you differentiate between yellow and blue by seeing, don't you? How do you differentiate between good and bad?"

"On the basis of feeling – what else?" Mr Russell weakly replied.

The obvious weakness of this response is that feelings can be manipulated. Hitler and his Nazis had the majority support of the German people in the 1930s.

Some cultures love their neighbours; in other cultures they eat them, both on the basis of feeling.[90]

Some have suggested that the problem of evil in the world is an argument against there being a God. A Christian speaker, after giving a lecture at Nottingham University, was asked whether the presence of evil in the world did not undermine the concept of an omnipotent God,

"There is too much evil in this world, therefore there cannot be a God." The speaker replied,

"When you say there is evil, aren't you admitting there is good? When you accept the existence of goodness, you must affirm a moral law on the basis of which to differentiate between good and evil. But when you admit to a moral law, you must point to a moral lawgiver. That, however, is what you are trying to disprove and not prove. For if there is no moral lawgiver, there is no moral law. If there is no moral law, there is no good, there is no evil. What then is your question?"[91]

It appears that all people have an innate instinct that there is right and there is wrong. Love, honesty and kindness towards us are valued, yet there is also something we call 'evil' in this world. Similarly, people do instinctively feel that their life has some value and purpose. Where do such values come from? These innate instincts do suggest that there is a 'creative superintendent'. The Bible's explanation is that we have all been made in the image of God. As he put these instincts into us so they are real and important. Without God such values must be artificial.

The Times columnist, Matthew Parris, is an atheist but he also recognises these moral instincts in all people that point to there being a deeper meaning in life.

"Inbred in me and all humans is an inescapable feeling that what comes after us matters. This is the eternal clash between simple observation – that for each of us everything is coming to an end – and one of our deepest instincts: that this cannot be all there is. There has to be something: we feel it in our very marrow."'[92]

---

[90] 'Can Man Live without God?' Word, 1995, p 325
[91] 'Can Man Live without God?' Word, 1995, p 325–326
[92] Quoted by Peter May, 'The Search for God and the Path to Persuasion', Malcolm Down Publishing, p.102

Guilt and Evil

The feeling of guilt is interesting, shouting that there is right and wrong in the world and in us. Guilt is, to some degree a universal phenomenon. Although some people with obsessive personalities are liable to be overwhelmed with excessive feelings of guilt, this should not negate its significance. I have an instinct within me that I should do what is right and when I do something wrong or fail to do something right, something inside my conscience hurts. When Potiphar's wife was trying to seduce Joseph, he replied.

"How then could I do such a wicked thing and sin against God." Genesis 39:9

Joseph recognised that guilt was not just the effect of social upbringing, but was a God given instinct that we have all been given to help us search for and stay close to God.

International law reflects the ethical teaching of the Bible. Jacques Derrida, the atheistic French philosopher has recognised this,

"Today the cornerstone of international law is…the sacredness of man as your neighbour…made by God. In that sense, the concept of crime against humanity is a Christian concept and I think there would be no such thing in the law today without the Christian message, the Abrahamic heritage, the Biblical heritage.[93]"

There are many today who consider that guilt is just the effect of social conditioning. Undoubtedly conditioning can influence our feelings of guilt but is there an absolute aspect to right and wrong, which is what the Bible teaches, or are all moral values the effect of our upbringing? If our moral values are solely conditioned by our environment then there is no real concept of right and wrong. The philosopher Friedrich Nietzsche had declared,

"When one gives up Christian belief one thereby deprives oneself of the right to Christian morality. Christianity is a system, a consistently thought out and complete view of things. If one breaks out of it a fundamental idea, the belief in God, one thereby breaks the whole thing to pieces: one has nothing of any consequence left in one's hands. Christian morality is a command: its origin is

---

[93] In 'Questioning God', edited by John D. Caputo, Mark Dooley, Michael J. Scanlon p.70

transcendental, it possesses truth only if God is truth – it stands or falls with belief in God."[94]

One of the greatest difficulties many modern people have is finding a unity between their instincts on right and wrong and modern ways of thinking. This is the consequence of our conditioning. Modern philosophies have killed off God and consequently have removed the concept of sin. However it cannot remove the subjective reality of sin. This is engrained into our instincts.

In Washington, the Managing Editor of what is probably the city's most prestigious political weekly was a post-modernist thinker. Martha (not her real name) regarded all constructions of good and evil as social structures without any absolute force. So she thought that although the Jewish holocaust looked pretty ghastly from a Jewish perspective, for those committed to an Aryan theory it looked like the way to go. She considered that morality depended on your point of view, whether you are talking about the tribal conflicts in Rwanda or other more recent conflicts such as those in Ukraine or the Middle East. She felt you could construct concepts of evil and good out of the social matrix of where you live.

At this time, Martha got to know Mark and Connie Dever. Mark is the senior pastor of Capitol Hill Baptist Church. They invited her to come to a Bible Study in their home. She noted that they handled the text well and because she was interested in words and texts she went along. However she did not agree with what was said, considering it mostly to be a load of 'poppycock'. She did not know much about the Bible so she went along and learned all the 'stuff about Jesus' from the gospel of Mark, even though she did not believe it. It was just an interesting handling of the texts as far as she was concerned.

Martha was then sent on an assignment to Papua New Guinea (PNG) for political reasons. Just as she was about to leave that country she came across the story of a priest who had been arrested for paedophilia. He was about to return home for retirement after spending thirty five years in PNG. It transpired that he had sodomised no fewer than two hundred children over those thirty five years. She could not stop thinking about this man and the possible consequences of his actions. She thought about all the relationships his behaviour would touch. What would happen to those children when they grew up? How many of them would

---

[94] Friedrich Nietzsche, 'Twilight of the Idols'

become abusers themselves? Would they ever be able to have happy marriages? These issues grabbed her.

When she returned to Washington, she discussed it all with Mark Dever. Mark's response was to ask,

"Martha, was it wicked?"

Martha replied,

"Come on, Mark, we all know that the vast majority of child abusers were themselves abused as children. This sort of thing gets passed on, doesn't it? They are as much victims as victimisers."

Mark smiled,

"True enough. That's what the Bible says too. Sin is social as well as personal. 'Sins of the fathers will be visited upon the children to the third and fourth generation of those who hate me.' There are few private sins. That is not the issue. The issue is, "Was it wicked?"'"

Martha could not get away from this question. When she bumped into Mark on the street, he would say,

"Hi, Martha, was it wicked?"

When she went to the Bible study, she would be greeted with,

"Hi, Martha. Welcome. Was it wicked?"

Every time Mark saw her he asked,

"Was it wicked?"

Martha could not sleep. Her instincts and her philosophy were in conflict. She would wake up in the middle of the night and would hear Mark's voice saying,

"Was it wicked?"

Then one night she woke up in the middle of the night. She couldn't sleep. She was sweating by the side of her bed as she wrestled with the same question. Then she concluded,

"This was wicked. This was wicked. This was very wicked."

Then it dawned on her,

"Maybe I'm wicked too."[95]

Martha's gut instincts had overcome her atheistic way of thinking. She now recognised that evil is an offence primarily against God and she was not without

---

[95] This account was taken from a talk by Don Carson to the Christian Medical Fellowship annual student conference in February 2003

fault in that regard. Within three weeks, she had become a Christian. It now all made sense, her instincts and rational thinking were united. Now she is one of the most able communicators of the gospel in Washington. It all makes sense.

No one asks for pardon till they know they are guilty. No one asks for life until they are under the sentence of death. You don't ask God for forgiveness until you know you are wicked. Nothing will satisfy the void in peoples' lives until they realise they are devoid of God.

Our generation's attempts to generalise and rationalise all evil, particularly in ourselves, has the effect of domesticating the gospel. It becomes diluted and weakened. We don't need forgiveness but help to deal with the issues. The cross has become devoid of meaning. Jesus came to die so that I can be forgiven but we prefer some form of psychotherapy to deal with every issue, even the sin that separates me from God.

Sin

At heart, sin is the innate rebellion against God that we all suffer from. It is spelt 's I n', emphasising with great clarity that the root of sin is the 'I' placed at the centre of my motivation. 'Sins', as opposed to 'sin' are those things we do wrong as a result of this rebellion, we lie, cheat, say unkind things, lust and the like. This is different from, but related to, guilt. We may sin and not feel particularly guilty. The more we go against our consciences the less we are concerned. It is as if our conscience is a square piece of wood on a rotating lathe. When the chisel first approaches the wood, it jars as the corners of the wood are repeatedly contacted, but gradually, as the chisel eats into the wood there is much less jarring. So our consciences can be weakened by repeated rejection over time. Romans chapter 1 confirms that all men are culpable before God because we reject the truths he has put into our instincts.

"The wrath of God is being revealed from heaven against all the godlessness and wickedness of people, **who suppress the truth by their wickedness** since **what may be known about God is plain to them, because God has made it plain to them**. For since the creation of the world God's invisible qualities – his eternal power and divine nature – have been clearly seen, being understood from what has been made, so that people are without excuse.

For although they knew God, they neither glorified him as God nor gave thanks to him, but their thinking became futile and their foolish hearts were darkened. Although they claimed to be wise, they became fools and exchanged the glory of the immortal God for images made to look like a mortal human being and birds and animals and reptiles.

Therefore God gave them over in the sinful desires of their hearts to sexual impurity for the degrading of their bodies with one another. **They exchanged the truth about God for a lie, and worshipped and served created things rather than the Creator** – who is forever praised. Amen." Romans 1:18–25

Suffering

When I was working as a surgeon, I had an interest in treating patients with cancer, I would often ask them,

"Do you have a faith that helps you at a time like this – or aren't you sure about these things."

Too often the reply came back,

"I wish I had."

For some this deep-felt need led them to investigate and then put their trust in Christ. Suffering has strange effects on people. Some are drawn to God but others use it as a reason for turning away from him, questioning how a good God can allow them to suffer.

In Buddhism, existence and suffering go together. The main question that Guatama (c.566 BC–c.480 BC), the traditional founder of Buddhism, sought to answer was: "Why do pain and suffering exist?" His solution was to try and reach a mental state where suffering is no longer a problem.

In contrast, the Bible acknowledges that suffering is a major feature of life but claims that it has a purpose – to draw us back to God so that we realise our dependence on him[96]. Jesus entered this world and suffered with us in it in many different ways. God is not aloof but is able to sympathise with us and give us hope even when we are dying. The late Christian thinker, John Stott, treasured this aspect of Jesus.

"I could never myself believe in God if it were not for the cross. In the real world of pain, how could one worship a God who was immune to it? I have entered many Buddhist temples…and stood respectfully before the statue of the Buddha, his legs crossed, arms folded, eyes closed, the ghost of a smile

---

[96] Luke 13:1–5

playing around his mouth…detached from the agonies of the world. But each time, after a while, I have had to turn away. And in my imagination I have turned instead to that lonely, twisted, tortured figure on the cross, nails through hands and feet, back lacerated, limbs wrenched, brow bleeding from thorn-pricks, mouth dry and intolerably thirsty, plunged in God-forsaken darkness. That is God for me! He laid aside his immunity to pain. He entered our world of flesh and blood, tears and death. He suffered for us."[97]

John Williams worked in the City of London and was an avid reader. He arranged for 'Penguin' to send him all their new publications. One day he received 'The Four Gospels, a new translation by Dr E.V. Rieu'. He read from this every morning and evening as he travelled into his office. One day he travelled home late at night so he settled into a corner of the train carriage and continued to read Luke's gospel. He had got as far as Luke's account of the crucifixion.

There were two other men in the compartment, one was an Englishman and the other an American. The Englishman suddenly had a fit and fell to the floor. The American jumped up and expertly loosened the man's tie and put his handkerchief in his mouth to stop him biting his tongue.

"I'm awfully sorry, but this happens several times a week. You see, we were in the Korean war together, I was wounded and left in no-man's land and this Englishman came and carried me to safety. Just as we were arriving at a safe position, a shell landed beside us and the next thing we knew was that we were in hospital. I was invalided out of the army back to America when I heard that the Englishman would never get better. I left my job, broke off my engagement and came to England to look after him. You see, he did it for me. There is nothing that I cannot do for him."

The two left the carriage at the next stop and John Williams continued reading about the crucifixion, but those words kept resonating round his mind,

"He did that for me, there is nothing that I cannot do for him."

Suddenly John Williams closed his book, knelt in the compartment and gave his life to Christ. This is the decision that all Christians have made.[98] The apostle Peter said that Christ died 'to bring you to God' (1 Peter 3:18).

---

[97] John Stott, 'The Cross of Christ', Nottingham IVP, 2006, p. 335–336
[98] Recounted by Ian Barclay in 'The Facts of the Matter', Falcon 1977. 21–22

For those who are in Christ, there is a sure future as this same God who entered this fallen world will return to establish a perfect real world where he rules with love and fairness. The apostle John describes this.

"Then I saw a new heaven and a new earth, for the first heaven and the first earth had passed away…I heard a loud voice from the throne saying, 'Now is the dwelling of God with men, and he will live with them. They will be his people, and God himself will be with them. They will be his people, and God himself will be with them and be their God. He will wipe away every tear from their eyes. There will be no more death or morning or crying or pain, for the old order of things has passed away. He who was seated on the throne said, 'I am making everything new.'" Revelation 21:1–5

It is only by beginning with God that we can adequately explain these values within us.

Chapter 15
The God-Shaped Gap

The philosopher and mathematician, Blaise Pascal argued that the human experience of emptiness and the yearning for something more is an indication that our essential need is to be fulfilled in something greater – a relationship with the God who made us. Pascal became a Christian when he was aged 31.

Augustine expressed this in his famous prayer,

"You have made us for yourself and our heart is restless until it finds its rest in you."

C.S. Lewis also argued that there is a God-shaped gap within all people that we try to satisfy in many different ways – usually by inventing our own false, temporary gods. In the absence of God, people experience a deep sense of longing, a longing that is really for God but is misinterpreted as a longing for things in this world.

The Message of the Apostles

Jesus' apostles always emphasised the need for teaching people. They did this because they perceived faith in Jesus to be based on reason. In Peter's first sermon at Pentecost, he taught them about the life, death and resurrection of Jesus. He showed how the Old Testament Scriptures had foretold these events. Many of his listeners' consciences were awakened and three thousand accepted his message and made an open commitment to Christ. It is significant that their rulers had just arranged for this same Christ to be crucified seven weeks earlier, so Peter's listeners must have been convinced, as well as convicted, to have made such a commitment.

It was what the apostles were teaching about the life, death and resurrection of Christ, and their emphasis that this was all foretold in Scripture, that put the authorities in a difficult position. They did not like the conclusion but could not argue against the evidence. It was the content of their message, not the way it was delivered that concerned the priests and the ruling Sadducees.

"They were greatly disturbed because the apostles were teaching the people and proclaiming in Jesus the resurrection of the dead…but many who **heard the message** believed." Acts 3:2–4

The apostles based their message on the evidence of what they had 'seen and heard' (Acts 4:20), supported by the Old Testament prophecies about the Christ.

"Day after day, in the temple courts and from house to house, **they never stopped teaching and proclaiming the good news that Jesus is the Christ.**" Acts 5:42

This remained Paul's approach – he used rational arguments to persuade people about Jesus. When he arrived in Athens, his approach remained that of trying to persuade people about who Jesus was.

"So **he reasoned** in the synagogue with the Jews and the God-fearing Greeks, as well as in the market place day by day with those who happened to be there." Acts 17:17

"Paul was **preaching the good news about Jesus and the resurrection**." Acts 17:18

When he went to Corinth on his Second Missionary journey, he continued in trying to convince people that Jesus was the Christ.

"Every Sabbath he reasoned in the synagogue, **trying to persuade** Jews and Greeks." Acts 18:4

This appears to have been the approach of all the early Christians. Apollos was a scholar who had a thorough knowledge of the Scriptures. When he visited Achaia, the region around Corinth, in Greece,

"He **vigorously refuted** the Jews in public debate, **proving from the Scriptures** that Jesus was the Christ." Acts 18:28

When Paul was defending himself before King Agrippa II against Jewish accusations, it became clear to the king that Paul was trying to convince him and his sister Bernice about the truth of the Christian message. Paul gave his testimony, explaining how he had become convinced about Jesus, having previously been violently opposed to him. Part of the evidence he used was that subjective instinct that tells us that we are not what God made us to be. He then talked about the need for all people to repent and turn to God, proving their repentance by the new way they lived. His final argument was that of Scripture. The Old Testament prophets foretold that the Christ would die and then rise from the dead. They also teach that this good news would be preached to Gentiles as well as Jews. It was this last point that was the basis of the Jewish accusations against Paul.

"I am saying nothing beyond what the prophets and Moses said would happen – that the Christ would suffer and, as the first to rise from the dead, would proclaim light to his own people and to the Gentiles." Acts 26:22–23

Doubtless this account in Acts 26 is a summary of what Paul actually said to the king. Agrippa was well acquainted with Jewish customs and controversies and would have known of the stories about Jesus that had been circulating. I fully suspect that Paul would have elaborated on and quoted some of the Old Testament Scriptures he was referring to as Paul's great learning was then acknowledged by Agrippa,

"Your great learning is driving you insane." Acts 2624

Paul continues to argue the validity of his case. His faith in Jesus was evidence based. His reply is striking,

"What I am saying is **true and reasonable**. The King is familiar with these things, and I can speak freely to him. I am convinced that none of this has escaped his notice, because it was not done in a corner." Acts 26:25

It was only when he had given the reasons that he explains that a decision has to be made. The decision Paul wants Agrippa to make was not primarily about whether he had broken the law but about the validity of Jesus' claims.

"King Agrippa, do you believe the prophets? I know you do." Acts 26:27

Paul's argument was clear. He was basing his defence of the validity of Jesus Christ's claims, which the Jewish Scriptures support. Agrippa understood this, saying to Paul.

"Do you think in such a short time you can persuade me to be a Christian?" Acts 26:28

Paul acknowledges that this is his purpose, he clearly thinks all people, including those present in the court that day, needed to be convinced about who Jesus was, because their eternal salvation depended on it.

Paul replied, "Short time or long – I pray God that not only you but all who are listening to me today may become what I am, except for these chains." Acts 26:29

Clearly Paul wants all people to become as convinced about Jesus as he is, and as a result to become followers of Jesus.

This apostolic technique of evangelism never changed. When Paul arrived in Rome, after he had appealed to Caesar, he was allowed to rent his own house though still under a Roman guard. He quickly arranged to see the leaders of the Jewish community in Rome so he could explain to them why he had been arrested and why he had appealed to Caesar.

"They arranged to meet Paul on a certain day and came in even larger numbers to the place where he was staying. From morning till evening, he explained and declared to them the kingdom of God and tried **to convince them** about Jesus from the Law of Moses and from the prophets. Some were **convinced** by what he said but others would not believe." Acts 28:23–24

The sort of evidence Paul used and his approach differed depending on whom he was talking to, but he was always trying to convince people that Jesus was the one and only Son of God. This was proved by his life, death and resurrection as well as the Jewish Scriptures that prophesied many specific details about God's Messiah's birth, death, resurrection and the purpose of his coming. He was to be God's final sacrifice for our sin so that we can be saved.

When John wrote his gospel, he carefully described seven of Jesus' miracles as well as his teaching. It was this factual evidence about Jesus that was presented so that people may put their trust in him. Towards the end of his gospel he writes,

"Jesus did many other miracles in the presence of his disciples, which are not recorded in this book. **But these are written that you may believe that Jesus is the Christ, the Son of God, and that by believing you may have life in his name.**" John 20:30–31

The message of the church can never change. Jesus is the one and only Son of God. The Bible makes clear that Jesus is God, the creator of our universe but that he has entered this world as a person. This is a staggering claim but beginning with God is the key to making sense of life and giving our lives a certain purpose.

Chapter 16
The Consequences of Rejecting God

When Paul wrote to the church in Rome, he reminded them why sharing the news about Jesus is vital.

"I am not ashamed of the gospel, because it is **the power of God for the salvation of everyone who believes**." Romans 1:16

Salvation for him meant being made right with God. He goes on to stress that those who reject Jesus and his gospel do so for false reasons. It is this rejection that makes God angry:

"The wrath of God is being revealed against all the godlessness and wickedness of men who suppress the truth by their wickedness…" Romans 1:18

God's wrath is not a petulant, irrational anger, such as humans can demonstrate, but a well-reasoned and rational wrath. That God matters should be clear for the following reasons:

Evidence from nature

Paul continues to explain why those who reject God's claims deserve God's judgment:

"…**since what may be known about God is plain to them**. For since the creation of the world God's invisible qualities, his eternal power and divine nature have been clearly seen, being understood by what has been made, so that men are without excuse." Romans 1:18–19

They overlooked the clear design and beauty of creation. Today we have even less excuse because the complexities of DNA and cell structures should lead us all to worship our creator. We don't know how he created this world but it is clearly designed. Eyes, ears and taste did not develop haphazardly!

"Although they claimed to be wise, they became fools and exchanged the glory of the immortal God for…" Romans 1:22–23

Don't you wonder at how people are made and can think? Professor John Lennox has astutely concluded:

"Either human intelligence ultimately owes its origin to mindless matter, or there is a creator. It is strange that some people claim that it is their intelligence that leads them to prefer the first to the second."[99]

Evidence from morality

When individuals forsake God, they and their society eventually forsake righteous living. Immorality becomes a common feature. Isn't this what we are seeing in the West today? The Romans made statues of famous men or animals and then worshipped them as idols because they revered certain qualities seen in them. Today everyone worships someone or something – anything can take the place of God such as power, fame, careers, money, and sex. Some think our immoral behaviour is the reason God is angry, but this passage says that God is primarily angry because men have forgotten him – the sexual depravities are simply symptoms of this rejection and that God has taken the brakes off, brakes that control a society.

"Because of this, God gave them over to shameful lusts. Even their women exchanged natural relations for unnatural ones. In the same way, the men also abandoned natural relations with women and were inflamed with lust for one another." Romans 1:26–27

Are we not seeing this today with many sections of society promoting promiscuous sexual activities? Sexual immorality is not the only symptom of what happens when people turn their backs on God. This list is horrific, they nearly all are to do with failed interpersonal relationships:

"Furthermore, just as they did not think it worthwhile to retain the knowledge of God, so God gave them over to a depraved mind, so that they do what ought not to be done. They have become filled with every kind of wickedness, evil, greed and depravity. They are full of envy, murder, strife, deceit and malice. They are gossips, slanderers, God-haters, insolent, arrogant and boastful; they

---

[99] John Lennox, 'God's Undertaker: Has Science Buried God?', p. 210

invent ways of doing evil; they disobey their parents; they have no understanding, no fidelity, no love, no mercy." Romans 1:29–31

Isn't it obvious that there is a natural link between how people treat others and how they treat God.

Evidence from our consciences

Deep down all people know that to behave in such ways is wrong and that they are guilty before the judgment seat of God. Paul emphasises this,

"Although they know God's righteous decree that those who do such things deserve death, they not only continue to do these very things but also approve those who practice them." Romans 1:32

All people, not just religious Jews, have God-given consciences. Later Paul says:

"Indeed, when Gentiles, who do not have the law, do by nature things required by the law, they are a law for themselves, even though they do not have the law, since they show that the **requirements of the law are written on their hearts, their consciences also bearing witness**, and their thoughts now accusing, now even defending them." Romans 2:14–15

There is something deep inside all of us that recognises spiritual realities.

Frank Jenner was a very polite, charming elderly Australian living in Sydney. He was a retired sailor. Every day he would go down to George Street looking for people he might talk to. He did this for thirty years and must have talked to around 100,000 people. Corporal Murray Wilkes was in a hurry to catch a tram on George St when a voice behind him called,

"Hey, wait!"

The well-dressed stranger then politely asked,

"Soldier, if you were to die tonight where would you go? Would it be heaven or hell?"

"I hope I'd go to heaven," the corporal replied.

"Hoping isn't enough, you can know for sure."

This stranger's question resonated through Murray Wilkes mind over the following days. He was a married, church-going man but he also knew that he was a hypocrite who had never seriously thought about his eternal destiny. He started to ask questions. Two weeks later Murray knelt in his army barracks and gave his life to Christ. This simple question has stirred many people's consciences and helped them search for answers to the meaning of life because it resonates with an instinctive feeling.

Evidence from our criticism of others

In a Peanuts cartoon, Linus is curled up in a chair, reading a book, while Lucy stands behind him with a funny look on her face. Lucy then says,

"It's very strange. It happens just by looking at you."

"What happens?" Linus asks.

Lucy calmly answers, "I can feel a criticism coming on."

God is perfectly just in in his judgments because we do naturally criticise others who behave in ways we disapprove of:

"You therefore, have no excuse, you who pass judgment on someone else, for at whatever point you judge the other, you are condemning yourself, because you who pass judgment do the same thing." Romans 2:1

People may try to rationalise their behaviour and that of others. However it is clear that every one of us is culpable before God and will be judged accordingly,

"This will take place on the day when **God will judge men's secrets through Jesus Christ**." Romans 2:16

The next chapter confirms this doctrine that there is no-one who can stand before God on the judgment day, the only escape will be to be forgiven.

"This **righteousness from God comes through faith in Jesus Christ to all who believe**. There is no difference, for **all have sinned** and fall short of the glory of God, and are justified freely by his grace through the redemption that came by Christ Jesus." Romans 3:22–23

This the same message throughout the Bible. The prophet Isaiah said:

"Turn to me and be saved, all you ends of the earth; for I am God, and there is no other." Isaiah 45:22

This was the verse that a 15 year old Charles Hadden Spurgeon heard on a cold night in a small village Methodist chapel near Colchester. One Sunday morning, early in January, he was making his way to one church when a fierce snow storm led him, instead, to enter the Primitive Methodist Chapel located closer to his home. Only about a dozen people were there that morning, and he took a seat near the back, under the gallery.

The regular minister had not been able to come due to the storm. So, when it was time for the sermon, a thin man, whom Spurgeon supposed to be a shoemaker or a tailor, went up to the pulpit. He announced and read the Scripture text for his impromptu sermon, Isaiah 45:22:

"Look unto me, and be ye saved, all the ends of the earth."

The man obviously had little formal education, and he mispronounced some of his words. But that did not matter to Spurgeon, for upon hearing the Bible verse he thought it contained a glimmer of hope for him.

The lay preacher began to deliver a homespun discourse in his broad Essex dialect:

"This is a very simple text indeed. It says, 'Look.' Now lookin' don't take a deal of pain. It ain't lifting your foot or your finger; it is just 'Look.' Well, a man needn't go to college to learn to look. You may be the biggest fool, and yet you can look. A man needn't be worth a thousand pounds a year to look. Anyone can look; even a child can look."

But then the text says, "Look unto Me." Ay! many on ye are looking to yourselves, but it's no use lookin' there. You'll never find any comfort in yourselves. Some say look to God the Father. No, look to Him by-and-by. Jesus Christ says, "Look unto Me." Some on ye say, "We must wait for the Spirit's working." You have no business with that just now. Look to Christ. The text says, "Look unto Me." Assuming the perspective of Jesus, the preacher continued:

"Look unto Me; I am sweatin' great drops of blood. Look unto Me; I am hangin' on the cross. Look unto Me, I am dead and buried. Look unto Me; I rise again. Look unto Me; I ascend to Heaven. Look unto Me; I am sitting at the Father's right hand. O poor sinner, look unto Me! Look unto Me!"

After he had spoken for about ten minutes, the layman apparently reached the end of his sermon. Then, fixing his eyes on Spurgeon, he startled him by saying,

"Young man, you look very miserable. And you will always be miserable – miserable in life and miserable in death – if you don't obey my text. But if you obey now, this moment, you will be saved." Then raising his hands, he literally shouted: "Young man, look to Jesus Christ. Look! Look! Look! You have nothing to do but look and live!"

Far from taking offence at being singled out, Spurgeon at once saw the way of salvation. He hardly noticed anything the lay exhorter said after that, so taken was he with that one thought:

"I had been waiting to do fifty things, but when I heard that word – Look! – what a charming word it seemed to me. There and then the cloud was gone, the darkness had rolled away and that moment I saw the sun. And I could have risen that instant, and sung with the most enthusiastic of them, of the precious blood of Christ, and the simple faith which looks alone to Him. Oh, that somebody had told me this before, 'Trust Christ, and you shall be saved'."[100]

The young Spurgeon recognised that Jesus was the answer to his needs and he put his faith in Christ. He then went on to become one of the greatest preachers in the Victorian era.

---

[100] http://vancechristie.com/2018/07/19/look-to-christ-and-live-charles-spurgeons-conversion/

Chapter 17
Can the Gospels Be Trusted?

In a recent conversation, a student expressed a deep concern,
"I really admire the teaching of Jesus and his church but I still have a nagging concern, 'Is this whole story really true?"

So much depends on the reliability of the four gospel writers.[101] They are like four witnesses in a court of law. Their evidence concerns Jesus, a man who has changed the world and continues to do so. Consequently, it is vital to answer this question. Are the gospels still reliable, can we believe what they say? This question can be sub-divided into,

a. Authorship – are they first-hand accounts originating from the apostles?
b. Believable – are they accurate accounts of what Jesus said and did?
c. Copying – have they been reliably passed on?
d. Divine – are they the word of God for today?

For Jesus to claim to be the incarnation of God, his one and only Son, to have performed such extraordinary miracles such as healing paralysed and blind people and raising the dead, to say that he would also rise to life after being put to death and then to do so is so outside our normal experience that such claims need to be substantiated. There is very strong external evidence from documents and artefacts outside the Bible and internal evidence within the writings themselves to confirm that these witnesses were telling the truth. Furthermore, there is subjective evidence that we can experience for ourselves as to how these books, that claim to be the Word of God, have helped to change people from

---

[101] I am grateful to the article by Dr F. David Farnell, "Are the gospels reliable" https://defendinginerrancy.com/are-the-gospels-reliable/

being selfish individuals into becoming more fulfilled, purposeful and godly team members.

Let us start by investigating the early manuscripts, looking at the evidence for their authorship and whether there is good evidence that they accurately described the life and sayings of Jesus. This case for the trustworthiness of the New Testament is often contrasted with other important ancient, classical Greek and Roman writings, which, although they do not exhibit the same wealth of substantiating data of early documents are still considered to be genuine records of events.

Earliest Manuscripts

Although we do not have any of the original documents, we do have copies made less than a hundred years later. There is a small manuscript of a portion of Mark's gospel copied during the second century AD which is in the Rylands Library in Manchester and contains just 4 verses from John's gospel. This is dated around 150AD. In the Bodmer Library in Geneva, there is a manuscript containing most of John's gospel that was also written around 150AD. Another small fragment contains a few letters on each side from verses 7–9 and 16–18 of Mark chapter 1. On the basis of the handwriting, this was written around 150–250 AD. The manuscript itself is tiny, only 4.4 x 4 cm. Lines of writing preserved on each side indicate that this fragment comes from the bottom of the first written page of a codex – a book rather than a scroll.

There are also over 30 papyrus codices, or books as opposed to scrolls, that were copied in the 2nd, 3rd and 4th centuries. In the Chester Beatty Library in Dublin, there is a papyrus codex of the four gospels and the book of Acts which is dated as being early third century. The Codex Vaticanus and Codex Sinaiticus originally contained both Old and New Testaments and are dated around 350AD.

The early Church Fathers quoted extensively from the gospels, apostolic letters and the Old Testament. Irenaeus wrote in the middle of the second century and he often quotes from Old and New Testaments. Even earlier, 1 Clement is a letter which was written by Clement (died 99AD) from Rome to the church in Corinth during the first century AD. Some have dated it as early as the later 60s AD though most consider it to be late first century. The point is that Clement quotes from the New Testament considerably and many of the basic doctrines of the Christian faith are clearly taught, including the divinity of Christ, justification, and a reliance upon inerrant Scriptures. The church in Rome at around that time was using at least Matthew and Luke and several Pauline epistles including 1 Corinthians, Romans and Hebrews and they considered these apostolic writings to be authoritative. Ignatius, Bishop of Antioch, wrote a letter before his martyrdom in Rome in A.D. 115, quoting all the four gospels and other New Testament letters. Polycarp wrote to the Philippians in A.D. 120 and quoted from the gospels and New Testament letters. Justin Martyr (A.D. 150) quotes John 3. Church fathers of the early second century were familiar with the apostles' writings and quoted them as inspired Scripture.

The striking finding across all these early manuscripts is that there is relatively little variation between them, and even when they have been translated into different languages, the meaning and doctrines remain the same.

Dating of the Original Gospels

In any study, it is important to remain impartial when assessing the evidence. There is now very strong evidence that all four gospels were written during the first century. The public ministry of Jesus was between 29–33AD. The distinguished New Testament scholar, Prof. F.F. Bruce, gives strong evidence that the New Testament was completed by 100AD.[102] Most of the twenty-seven writings in the New Testament were completed twenty to forty years before this. Traditionally Mark is thought to be the first gospel to be written, around 60AD. Matthew and Luke follow, being written between 60–70AD; John is the final gospel, written between 90–100AD. The liberal scholar, John Robinson thinks that all four gospels were written before the destruction of Jerusalem in 70AD and this is strongly argued in his book *Redating the New Testament*. He said, "The wealth of manuscripts and above all the narrow interval of time between the writing and the earliest extant copies, make it by far the best attested of any ancient writing in the world."[103]

There is considerable internal evidence to support these early dates. The first three gospels prophesied the fall of the Jerusalem temple which occurred in 70AD, (see Matthew 24:1–25, Mark 13:1–4, 18–23 and Luke 21:5–7). However,

---

[102] F.F. Bruce, "The New Testament Documents: Are They Reliable?" 5th ed. (Downers Grove: InterVarsity Press, 1983), 14.

[103] John A.T. Robinson, "Can we Trust the New Testament?" (Grand Rapids: Eerdmans, 1977), 36.

none of them give even a hint that this destruction had happened. The most plausible explanation for this omission is that it had not yet occurred when these synoptic gospels were written.

Luke wrote the book of Acts as a follow on to his gospel. Similarly, the book of Acts repeatedly mentions the temple being in use in Jerusalem and yet again there is no hint that it no longer existed. There is no mention in the book of Acts or the gospels of the Jewish rebellion against Rome that started in 66AD. Luke describes Paul's house arrest in Rome but stops at that point. He does not mention his subsequent fourth missionary journey or the deaths of either Peter or Paul that probably occurred in 64AD. Putting this evidence together suggests that the book of Acts was written in 60AD, and the gospel of Luke was written slightly earlier.

The books in the New Testament were written and circulating so soon after the events recorded that there was no time for these written teachings to have been edited by the early Church. Sir Frederic G. Kenyon was the director of the British Museum (1889–1919) and in his book *The Bible and Archaeology*, he made the following statement about the existing Greek manuscripts of the New Testament:

"The interval then between the dates of original composition and the earliest extant evidence becomes so small as to be in fact negligible, and the last foundation for any doubt that the Scriptures have come down to us substantially as they were written has now been removed. Both the authenticity and the general integrity of the books of the New Testament may be regarded as finally established."[104]

Historian Christopher Blake speaks of the overlapping agreement of the early records, that together describe the truth, the 'very considerable part of history which is acceptable to the community of professional historians.'[105]

---

[104] Quoted in Josh McDowell, 'Evidence that Demands a Verdict,' Campus Crusade for Christ, 1972, 47
[105] Christopher Blake, "Can History be Objective?" in Gardiner, 331.

Dating of Early Christian Doctrines

The earliest Christian documents are thought to be the apostolic epistles we have in the New Testament. These contain the same message as the gospels about the divinity of Jesus and the Kingdom of God. A famous example is the list of Jesus' resurrection appearances supplied by Paul in 1 Corinthians 15:3–8. Most critical scholars think that Paul received the material on which this early creedal statement was written before 40AD.

Another argument for the authenticity of the gospels is the originality and unique teaching of Jesus. It was in many ways so different to that of the Jewish teachers of the time and brought a new way of understanding the Jewish Scriptures, our Old Testament. For example, Jesus introduced the term 'Abba' for God the Father which had not been previously used in Jewish writings. Where did this new teaching come from if not from Jesus?

Idiosyncrasies and Self-Criticisms

One feature of the gospels is the way the apostles are criticised and even criticise themselves. The denial of Jesus by Peter and the later criticisms over his early association with the circumcision party (Galatians 2:11–13), bear all the hallmarks of being early accounts, as he later became one of the first leaders of the church. Then James, Jesus' own brother, did not believe in Jesus' divinity prior to the crucifixion (Mark 3:20–25; John 7:5) but he later became the leader of the early church who was martyred by stoning in the 60's AD. Why did the gospel writers say that Jesus first appeared to Mary Magdalene and other women, when a woman's evidence was considered doubtful, if that did not actually happen? The difficulty the disciples had in accepting the resurrection similarly has 'the ring of truth' about it. Such arguments are the reasons why the majority of recent critical scholars believe that these are authentic firsthand reports.[106]

---

[106] Habermas, "The Risen Jesus and Future Hope," 21–22 provides some of the documentation.

Names and Grammar used in the Gospels[107]

If the gospels are authentic first century writings, then textual criticism can support or disprove this. A person writing in a later time period or from a different geographical area would inevitably get place names and other details wrong. Yet latest scholarship has supported that the wording used is contemporary with both excellent local geographical knowledge and word usage. The study of Jewish peoples' names in different countries and different generations shows that the gospels were written by people living in Israel during the first century AD. This has been discussed in more detail on page 123.

Evidence That the Gospels Are Factual Accounts

There are many details given in the gospels that demand that these are first-hand accounts. Specific names, dates and places are given and these have all been substantiated as being accurate. John described the healing of a paralysed man at the pool of Bethesda that he described as being,

"…surrounded by five covered colonnades." John 5:2

That pool was destroyed and covered with rubble when the Romans ransacked Jerusalem in 70AD. It was only excavated in the late 19th century. It has been found to consist of two adjacent pools that were surrounded on four sides by colonnades and an additional colonnade separated the two pools. Only someone who had visited the site prior to 70AD could have known this.

The apostles used to remind the crowds that they already knew many of the facts about Jesus. At Peter's first sermon, at Pentecost, given just seven weeks after the crucifixion of Jesus, he appealed to what they knew,

"Jesus of Nazareth was a man accredited by God to you by miracles, wonders sand signs which God did among you through him, **as you yourselves know**." Acts 2:22

At Paul's trial before King Agrippa and Festus, Paul was able to say,

"**What I am saying is true** and reasonable. **The king is familiar with these things**, and I can speak freely to him. I am convinced that none of this has escaped his notice because it was not done in a corner." Acts 26:25–26

---

[107] Peter Williams, https://www.youtube.com/watch?v=zTtdBpMMAFM

If there were any exaggerations or lies being told about Christ, contemporary witnesses could and would have discredited the apostles' accounts. They began preaching in the same cities as Jesus had taught in and during the lifetimes of many who had seen Jesus. When the early apostolic documents were circulating, there were many antagonists who would have picked on any errors with great glee. It was therefore essential that the gospel writers were very accurate in what they said. Those early Christians faced much opposition but there is no suggestion that any questioned the reliability of these documents.

The apostles and early Christians were widely known for their exemplary lifestyles and honesty. They faced incredible hardships for what they taught, they were beaten, ostracised, imprisoned, and many were killed because of their conviction that what they were taught about Jesus was true. They had no personal motives for lying or misrepresenting the teachings of Jesus. The major emphasis in their teaching was always on remaining truthful (such as Acts 5:3; Ephesians 4:25; Colossians 3:9; Revelation 22:15). The following are some examples of what the apostles taught concerning the reliability of what they have written.

Luke, the doctor and companion of Paul, who wrote the gospel of Luke and the book of Acts specifically states that he has personally checked the facts that others had recorded to ensure their validity. He said,

"Many have undertaken to draw up an account of the things that have been fulfilled among us, just as they were handed down to us by those who from the first were eyewitnesses and servants of the word. Therefore, since **I myself have carefully investigated everything from the beginning**, it seemed good also to me to write an orderly account for you, most excellent Theophilus, **so that you may know the certainty of the things you have been taught**." Luke 1:1–4

The apostle John wrote,

"The man who saw it has given testimony and **his testimony is true. He knows that he tells the truth**, and he testifies so that you also may believe." John 19:35

The apostle Peter wrote,

"**We did not follow cleverly invented stories** when we told you about the power and coming of our Lord Jesus Christ, but **we were eyewitnesses of his majesty**." 2 Peter 1:16

Remember these were men of integrity who lived and died for what they all taught. It is inconceivable that they were all liars and frauds. It is notable that no scholar in the last 80 years has doubted the sincerity of the early apostles.

Christians alive at the time of the apostles would have checked what was said and subsequent generations of Christian leaders claimed that they had passed on these teachings of the apostles accurately. Paul writing to Timothy, then leading the church in Ephesus, emphasised the need for keeping this chain of accurate teaching of God's truths to others continuing.

"And **the things you have heard me say in the presence of many witnesses entrust to reliable men** who will also be qualified to teach others. Endure hardship with us…" 2 Timothy 2:2–3

There is good evidence that this is how the early church leaders continued to behave. They were meticulous in checking that any documents presented to them were genuine apostolic writings before teaching from them. All these inspired writings were therefore early and carried certain apostolic authority.

Papias were born around. 65AD and died 135AD. It is thought that he knew the apostle John. He became the bishop of Hierapolis in Asia Minor. He wrote a five-volume work, around 130AD, called 'Expositions of the Sayings of the Lord' but only fragments of this work are known today, and this is only because of quotes by later writers.

The early church historian, Eusebius was born in 265 AD and became bishop of Caesarea from 315–340 AD. He quotes Papias as having said, "I will not hesitate to set down for you, along with my interpretations, everything I carefully learned then from the elders and carefully remembered, **guaranteeing their truth**."

And the Elder (either the apostle John or another leader in the early Church whose name was also John) used to say this: 'Mark, having become Peter's interpreter, wrote down **accurately** everything he remembered, though not in order, of the things either said or done by Christ. For he neither heard the Lord nor followed him, but afterward, as I said, followed Peter, who adapted his teachings as needed but had no intention of giving an ordered account of the Lord's sayings. Consequently, Mark did nothing wrong in writing down some things as he remembered them, for he made it his one concern not to omit anything which he heard **or to make any false statement in them**. So, Matthew composed the oracles in the Hebrew language…'

Polycarp was born around 69 AD and he faithfully passed on the apostolic teachings. He was a student of the apostle John and became bishop of Smyrna in Asia Minor. He was martyred for his faith. His student Irenaeus said significantly about him that:

"He always taught **what he learned from the apostles**, which the Church continues to hand on, and **which are the only truths.**"[108]

Irenaeus continued the tradition. Irenaeus (ca. 135–200) had also known Polycarp and later became bishop of Lyon in 177. He wrote the book *Against Heresies* in which he wrote,

"For we learned the plan of our salvation from no others than from those through whom the gospel came to us (the apostles). They first preached it abroad, and then later **by the will of God handed it down to us in Writings, to be the foundation and pillar of our faith**. So Matthew among the Hebrews issued a Writing of the gospel in their own tongue, while Peter and Paul were preaching the gospel at Rome and founding the Church. After their decease Mark, the disciple and interpreter of Peter, also handed down to us in writing what Peter had preached. Then Luke, the follower of Paul, recorded in a book the gospel as it was preached by him. Finally John, the disciple of the Lord…himself published the gospel."

In *Against Heresies,* Irenaeus is primarily concerned with heretical Gnostic teachings. Whilst Gnostics held a diversity of beliefs, in general they taught that they possessed secret traditions passed down from the apostles themselves, which they called 'apostolic tradition'. To counter this idea, Irenaeus appealed to the genuine 'apostolic tradition', the teachings written down in the New Testament and publicly taught by the apostles. 'Tradition', for Irenaus, meant the correct teaching and interpretation of Scripture, that contained the teachings that Jesus had passed on to his apostles. They, in turn, faithfully transmitted these to their students. This is the only genuine 'apostolic succession'. Irenaeus is saying that true doctrine is what Christ taught his disciples and that they taught their students, such as Clement of Rome, Ignatius of Antioch, Papias of Hierapolis and Polycarp of Smyrna. All these, in turn, taught subsequent generations the same message. In refuting Gnostic teachings, Irenaeus then refers to 'The Writings' or what we would now call 'the Scriptures,'

"But when they are refuted from the Writings they turn around and attack the Writings themselves, saying that they are not correct, or authoritative, and that the truth cannot be found from them by those who are not acquainted with the tradition [the secret gnostic teachings]. For this, they say, was not handed down in writing, but orally…" Against Heresies 3.2.1

---

[108] Irenaeus 'Against Heresies' book 3.1.1

"But when we appeal again to that tradition which has come down from the apostles and is guarded by the successions of elders in the churches, they oppose the tradition, saying they are wiser not only than the elders, but even than the apostles and have found the genuine truth." Against Heresies 3.2.2

"The tradition of the apostles, made clear in all the world, can be clearly seen in every church by those who wish to behold the truth. We can enumerate those who were established by the apostles as bishops in the churches, and their successors down to our time, none of whom taught or thought of anything like their mad ideas." Against Heresies 3.3.1

The authority of the church has always been the apostles and no sect or authority can change or add to this. It was very costly for these early church leaders to remain true to the faith as taught by the apostles and there is no suggestion at all that new, non-apostolic teaching should ever be accepted. This was later the central issue in the days of the Reformation, and the reformers such as Wyclif, Huss, Luther, Melanchthon, Zwingli, Calvin, Cranmer, Ridley and Latimer, all insisted that the church must continue to teach just what the apostles taught, nothing more and nothing less.

In a court of law, a witness is deemed to be reliable unless there is evidence to the contrary. When multiple witnesses affirm similar accounts, particularly when there are minor variations that help exclude collusion, the case for veracity can be confidently made. This is further strengthened when the witnesses have much to lose by persisting with their story.

The Gospels were referred to as being authoritative in other early respected Christian writings whose authorship is uncertain, such as *'The Epistle of Barnabas, The Shepherd of Hermas* and *The Didache'*. This is further evidence that the early church held the apostolic writings as definitive in matters of faith and doctrine.

Textual Variants

There are inevitably minor variations in the vast number (over 5,000) of early manuscripts, but these do not give rise to any doctrinal differences. In discussing the issue of variant readings, the scholar John Wenham has concluded that overall, the main Greek text, UBS4, used for translating the New Testament is 99.99 per cent pure, and without any differences affecting doctrine.[109] He said,

"The interesting and important thing about the late-second-century text is this: at that early date there was already a wide diversity of variants. These variants were of course mostly quite minor in character, but they show that there had been no recent systematic editing of the documents to make them conform to some standard version."[110]

Furthermore, Wenham believes that many of these variants go back to the first century and argues,

"Thus, the very existence of variants is itself powerful evidence against a systematic, tendentious alteration of the manuscripts in the very early stages of the history of the text."

Wenham concludes,

"Thus, from the minutely detailed study of the grammar and vocabulary of the early Greek texts of the New Testament there is no evidence to support the claims that the biblical text was tampered with by the early Church. The objectively verifiable evidence says just the opposite."

Non-Christian Writers

These have already been discussed in chapter 12. There are over eighteen early, non-biblical references to Jesus of Nazareth.[111] The details given in the writings of men such as Tacitus, Pliny the Younger and Suetonius strongly support what the apostles and the other early Christian writers describe.

Composition of the Synoptic Gospels

It does not take long to realise that there are many similarities between the first three gospels, because many verses are the same. Some have attributed this to an 'oral tradition'. People certainly did memorise long tracts of books and what people said but it does seem likely that people took notes of what Jesus had

---

[109] John Wenham, "Christ and the Bible" (Grand Rapids: Baker Books, 1984), 186–187.
[110] John Wenham, "Christ and the Bible,'" p. 178
[111] Gary R. Habermas, "The Historical Jesus: Ancient Evidence for the Life of Christ" (Joplin, MO: College Press, 1996), Chapter 9; F.F. Bruce, "Jesus and Christian Origins Outside the New Testament" (Grand Rapids: Eerdmans, 1974).

taught at the time and that the gospel writers used such notes. Some scholars have suggested that these were brought together in a script or many scripts called 'Q' which preceded the gospels. This would explain how Mark's gospel has 661 verses, 637 of which are reproduced in Matthew and/or Luke. Matthew and Luke share a further approximately 200 verses, which are not taken from Mark: these may have come from the 'Q' source.

Each of the gospel writers is writing for a different audience but their essential message is the same.

Further Corroborating Evidence

There is no doubt that a major factor that made people take note of Jesus was his claim to be the Son of God, the Messiah, combined with his ability to perform miracles. The Old Testament foresaw that the Messiah would perform miracles. For example, Isaiah foresaw that 'your God will come.'

"Then will the eyes of the blind be opened and the ears of the deaf unstopped. Then will the lame leap like a deer, and the mute tongue shout for joy." Isaiah 35:5–6

The four gospels all emphasise the miracles that Jesus performed, and it is impossible to rewrite them without this element. That these miracles really happened was widely recognised. The miracles of Jesus helped Nicodemus recognise that Jesus came from God,

"Rabbi, we know you are a teacher who came from God. **For no-one could perform the miraculous signs you are doing if God were not with him**." John 3:2

During the trials of Jesus, Pilate transferred him to see Herod.

"When Herod saw Jesus he was greatly pleased because for a long time he had been wanting to meet him. From what he had heard about him, he **hoped to see him perform some miracle**." Luke 23:8

In the early days of the church, the apostles demonstrated their authority by performing some miracles. It appears that this authenticating power to perform miracles was limited to the apostles.

"The **things that mark an apostle** – signs, wonders and miracles – **were done** among you with great perseverance." 2 Corinthians 11:12

It is significant that, except for the early epistle to the Corinthian church, miracles are not mentioned at all in subsequent apostolic letters. The letter to the Hebrews says that miracles were in the past.

"This salvation, which was first announced by the Lord, was confirmed to us by those who heard him. God also **testified** to it by signs, wonders and various miracles, and gifts of the Holy Spirit distributed according to his will." Hebrews 2:3–4

Early on, the significance of authenticating miracles was being minimised, even by the time of Paul's first letter to the Corinthians (around 55AD).

"Jews demand miraculous signs and Greeks look for wisdom but we preach Christ crucified." 1 Corinthians 1:22–23

It was the historical Christ, with his death and crucifixion, that the apostles emphasised. It was by teaching this that the church grew. Ever since the beginning this was their emphasis.

"Day after day, in the temple courts and from house to house, **they never stopped teaching** and proclaiming the good news that Jesus is the Christ." Acts 5:42

What the apostles taught about the historic Jesus was what the Old Testament Scriptures foresaw. It is significant that Paul substantiated what he taught about Jesus by showing that this is precisely what the Old Testament taught. When Paul first visited Thessalonica, his way of supporting the claims of the first hand witnesses was an appeal to the evidence of Scripture.

"…**he reasoned with them from the Scriptures, explaining and proving that the Christ had to suffer and rise from the dead.**" Acts 17:2–3

The 'noble' Berean Christians carefully checked what Paul had said to them,

"…for they received the message with great eagerness and examined the Scriptures every day **to see if what Paul said was true**." Acts 17:11

A friend of mine was blown away when he first read about the death and resurrection of Jesus as it is foretold in Isaiah 53:4–12, written 700 years before the Messiah entered this world. (This remarkable prophecy has been quoted on p 87) The death of the Messiah by crucifixion is described in gruesome detail in Psalm 22, even giving the detail of having his 'hands and feet pierced.' There are over 330 prophecies about the Messiah in the Old Testament that have been fulfilled by Jesus and these can still be checked today. The gospels describe how these prophecies were fulfilled by Jesus.

The Jewish Scriptures also describe in detail the heritage of God's Messiah. He would be a Jew, a descendant of Abraham, Isaac and Jacob. He would also be a descendant of Jesse and King David (Jeremiah 33:15). This is why the genealogy of Jesus given at the beginning of Matthew's gospel and in Luke chapter 3 give further corroborating evidence that what the gospels say about Jesus is really true.

The gospels cannot be dissociated from the Old Testament. Both talk about a supernatural historical Messiah, a real person who will reign for eternity, and both emphasise the moral implications of being admitted into God's kingdom, to be his chosen people.

Effect the Scriptures Have on People

Our godly instincts

A very strong further argument for the reliability of the gospels is that they speak of things that we inherently know to be true. The values that Jesus extols, honesty, kindness, love and his hatred of sin, such as pride, lust and coveting resonate with all people who value integrity. Integrity is the basis for all relationships. As we have seen, the opposite of 'integrity', which is doing what is right before God, is 'dis-integrity' or 'disintegration.' When individuals cease to value and act with integrity, their own lives begin to disintegrate, then their family, then their society and eventually their nation.

Our obedience

The followers of Jesus sometimes risked their lives because of the promises and instructions made in the Bible. One example is given above in the way Pliny treated Christians – he had them executed! This heroic cost was paid by men, women and even children who considered obedience to God to be their absolute priority. Christians were persuaded to obey these apostolic writings, knowing that the adherence to their contents could bring persecution or martyrdom. Jewish converts would never have placed any doubtful documents on equal standing with the authoritative books of the Old Testament if they were not convinced that they were also the word of God (see Matthew 5:17–19; Romans 3:2; 15:4; 1 Corinthians 10:1–11). Gentile converts, many well educated, would similarly have quickly rejected any documents whose dependability was uncertain, when the stakes were so high. The Gospels made strict moral demands and intelligent people would have devoted little attention to any literature that was suspect. The churches would never have allowed dubious compositions to circulate as God's Word as these were records upon which believers lived their lives and staked their eternal salvation.

When you look at how many people's lives today change for the better when they submit to the authority of God, there is clearly a power that is still made available through the Scriptures. **The same Spirit of God, who inspired the apostles to write the New Testament is at work in each of God's people to enable us to live as our Lord wants**.

A Roman Catholic priest in Belgium rebuked a young woman and her brother for reading that 'bad book', pointing to the Bible. She replied,

"Mr Priest, a little while ago my brother was an idler, a gambler, a drunkard and made such a noise in the house that no-one could stay in it. Since he began to read the Bible he works with industry, goes no longer to the pub, no longer touches cards, brings home money to his poor old mother and our life at home is quiet and peaceful. How comes it, Mr Priest, that a bad book produces such good fruits?"

The evidence that the gospels are indeed the 'Word of God' is very strong, both from objective (external) and subjective (internal) evidence. It therefore behoves all of us to take careful note of what Jesus teaches, as our eternal destiny is at stake. For these gospels teach us:

"Whoever believes in the Son has eternal life, but whoever rejects the Son will not see life, for God's wrath remains on him." John 3:36

This 'belief' that saves is more than just intellectual, it must involve a personal submission to Jesus Christ as my Lord and my Saviour. Becoming a Christian is like entering a permanent marriage, a marriage that will last through eternity.

The Apostle John's Assertion

What better way can there be than to read what the apostle John wrote in his old age about the Jesus he had known so well? John had committed his life to sharing the news about Jesus with the world, as he considered it to be so important. This opening paragraph to his first letter has the ring of honesty associated with urgency.

"That which was from the beginning, which **we have heard, which we have seen with our eyes, which we have looked at and our hands have touched – this we proclaim concerning the Word of life**. Life appeared; **we have seen it and testify to it** and we proclaim to you the eternal life, which was with the Father and has appeared to us. **We proclaim to you that we have seen and heard**, so that you also may have fellowship with us. And our fellowship is with the Father and with his Son, Jesus Christ. We write this to make our joy complete. **This is the message we have heard from him and declare to you: God is light; in him there is no darkness at all**." 1 John 1:1–5

Chapter 18
A Leap or Step of Faith?

I was recently talking with a politically active left wing couple who were atheists. They had thought that to be a Christian was an irrational leap into the dark. They had never heard of much of the evidence. We discussed the stepping stones to faith and significantly they were unable to come up with real answers to oppose the evidence. The problem they had was that they did not want God to have a say in how they lived and thought. They wanted to be independent. As they talked they reminded me of the issue facing Adam and Eve in the Garden of Eden. Would they continue to live under the authority of God or would they decide to make up their own morals and eat from the forbidden tree, 'the tree of knowledge of good and evil'. They also wanted to live independently of their creator.

The French mathematician and philosopher, Blaise Pascal, became a Christian when he was 31 years old. He wrestled with the question of why God is found by some and not others. This was his conclusion,

"Willing to appear openly to those who seek him with all their heart, and to be hidden from those who flee from him with all their heart, God so regulates the knowledge of himself that he has given indications of himself which are visible to those who seek him and not to those who do not seek him. There is enough light for those to see who only desire to see, and enough obscurity for those of a contrary disposition."

At the meal after the funeral of a friend, who had become a Christian, I was talking with one of his family about the faith of the deceased. He said, "But doesn't becoming a Christian demand a gigantic leap of faith?"

I replied, "I hope I can show you that to become a Christian does require a step of faith but that this is a small step based on a mass of evidence compared with the gigantic leap needed to reject Christ."

We discussed the two world scenarios of the two banks of the river and briefly went over the reasons for faith pictured as stepping stones across the river. He appeared to agree with the thinking behind each step. The universe does exist and the evidence is that it must have been designed, but that statement invokes the need for God. After a long time discussing the evidence, it was as if he was on the last of the stepping stones. He now had a different sort of choice to make, a moral choice. Was he willing for God to be his God? He recognised that to be a theoretical Christian only and not to live under the authority of His creator and his revealed Christ was not a tenable position, even though it is one so many hold. He went home to think!

People can either take a step of faith based on the objective evidence and our subjective instincts or take a massive leap of faith back into a selfish world where they are one of many gods. Logically to make such a massive leap should include providing answers to all the evidence provided by the stepping stones – but few bother to do this.

God requires us all to choose which world we want to live in but he warns us that this choice will have eternal consequences. It is much more than an intellectual exercise, our future depends on it.

"Whoever believes in the Son has eternal life but whoever rejects the Son will not see life for God's wrath remains on him." John 3:36

I don't think helping atheists is an issue for me

Some Christians may think that this is not a relevant topic for them as they are not in the habit of getting into conversation with non-Christians about spiritual matters. In a recent study in the United States, it was discovered that 8 out of 10 people, who claimed to be convinced Christians, had not talked with any non-Christians about the gospel or invited them to come with them to hear about the Christian message.

I will never forget going to a birthday party of a friend who had become a Christian. A good number of his work and music friends came, equalled by a number of church friends. Can you guess what happened? The church people all sat together on one side of the room and the non-Christians sat together on the other. Few crossed over to the other side. It was as if they had nothing important to share.

When Peter wrote to the early church, he recognised that some people were not able to explain their faith to others. He wrote,

"**Always** be prepared to give an answer to everyone who asks you to give the reason for the hope you have.1 Peter 3:15

The only way to be prepared is to do some prep! Some may need to be helped so they can comfortably talk to people they don't know well.

Didn't Jesus commission the church by saying, 'Therefore go and make disciples.'" Matthew 28:19

Too complacent

This will inevitably mean leaving our comfort zone in order to help others find Christ. One of the lessons we learnt very early on when I was at college was that Christians should not always sit together at mealtimes. We had to mix with non-Christians as we are here for Christ.

Too confrontational

Others are all too willing to get into religious discussions yet forget what the goal of a discussions should be – to make the message about the Lord Jesus eminently attractive. These people forget that arguments alone seldom win people. Indeed, winning the argument may well lead to the loss of a relationship and that can have eternal consequences. Surely this is why Peter adds a rider to the above,

"**But do this with gentleness and respect, keeping a clear conscience**, so that those who speak maliciously against your good behaviour in Christ may be ashamed of their slander."1 Peter 3:15–16

Today there seem to be two styles of evangelism. One is polemic antagonism – a head on pugilistic clash. This can only offend and is nearly always ineffective. The other is to gently get alongside someone, show them how much you have in common and gently steer them round to understand why we all need Christ and to the evidence that he really is the Saviour of the world.

Even in casual meetings a quick rapport can be built up as you talk about family, jobs and hobbies. You can quickly learn what matters to them and what concerns them. The key point in any conversation is to ask with genuine interest,

"Do you have a faith that helps you in this situation or aren't you sure about these things."

So often people will reply,

"I wish I had" or "I used to have" but others will reply, "I'm not sure it is true."

This last one is the topic of this book. It is an increasingly common issue and has great consequences.

Chapter 19
Why Is It So Hard to Change Your Mind?

Why do people find it so hard to become Christians when there is so much evidence that it is true?

There is much evidence from science that there has to have been a mind behind our creation. Who set the constants of the universe? Who designed the DNA system and code? How is it that our earth has exactly right properties that enable man to live on it? There is the evidence about Jesus and his life, teaching, miracles, his death and resurrection. There are many Old Testament prophecies that are fulfilled in him. What changed those early disciples so radically that they turned the world upside down within a generation? Philosophically we know that if our arguments start with man, we have nothing certain to live for or by but if we start with God we can find coherent answers. Furthermore, all humans have inherent spiritual instincts. We instinctively recognise that love, kindness, honesty, beauty and duty are real values although they cannot be proved. If we came accidentally from primordial soup, such values are artificial but if we are created in the image of God they can be explained and are real. However, in spite of such evidence, and there is much more than this, few people want to take that last step and become Christians.

David McRaney, a psychologist, has written a fascinating book *How Minds Change: The Surprising Science of Belief, Opinion and Persuasion*. In this book, he argues that people's beliefs, whether political, economic or religious, are seldom based on a cold evaluation of the facts, rather they are formed from the tribe we come from or the society we surround ourselves with. It seems that we are biologically hard-wired to keep believing whatever we already believe. He feels that facts rarely change people's minds. He describes an experiment where they put E.E.G electrodes on people's heads before they became engaged in a political discussion. When the arguments were going strongly against them they wouldn't change their minds, their brains just stopped working and they stopped listening.

It seems we are biologically wired up to keep believing what we already believe. Yet the Christian gospel calls on people to change their minds radically. 'Repent' literally means to 're-think', to rethink the direction of our lives. The Greek word for 'repent' is *meta-noia* which literally means 'a change of mind'.

What more is needed that will persuade people to recognise the significance of Jesus Christ so that their lives are permanently changed? Will it be spellbinding rhetoric in our pulpits, the ambiance of packed meetings or even irrefutable apologetics, a brilliant disclosure of the evidence that the message about Jesus is true. Even if such methods may have short-term effects Christian conversion is something much deeper – it is utterly life changing. Christian conversion is much more than hearing and agreeing, it is the doing that keeps on being done that matters. Jesus said, "Blessed are those who **hear the word of God and obey it.**" Luke 11:28

What a disaster it is when people who say they believe, live in ways that deny their so-called faith.

Jesus was quite willing to state publicly why many people would not believe in him, he says it is because we all have stubborn, sinful hearts. What stops our faith is not a lack of facts or information.

As the crowds increased, Jesus said, "**This is a wicked generation**. It asks for a sign, but none will be given it except **the sign of Jonah**. For as Jonah was a sign to the Ninevites, so also will the Son of Man be to this generation. The Queen of the South will rise at the judgment with the people of this generation and condemn them, for she came from the ends of the earth to listen to Solomon's wisdom; and now something greater than Solomon is here. The men of Nineveh will stand up at the judgment with this generation and condemn it, for they repented at the preaching of Jonah; and now something greater than Jonah is here." Luke 11:29–32

The Wicked Will Always Want More Evidence

In the original Greek of the above passage from Luke the phrase, 'It asks for a sign' is in the present continuous tense so it literally means, 'It keeps asking for a sign'. Up until this point in Luke's record of the life of Jesus he has described some of the many miraculous signs that Jesus had performed. Jesus had calmed the storm, showing he was Lord of the natural world, he had healed the deaf and lame, raised the dead and cast out demons, showing he was Lord over Satan. What more did his critics want. Even when he rose from the dead, as he had frequently foretold, many still would not believe in him.

Jesus encouraged people to look at the evidence supporting his claims, it is the abundance of this evidence that convinces us that his message is true. In John's gospel, there are three major sections where Jesus urges people to look at the evidence for his claims and these passages are worth studying (John 5:31–47, John 8:31–59 and John 10:22–42).

This crowd kept on asking for more and more evidence when reality was standing there before them. How much evidence did they need? There is a Chinese proverb that says,

"Man stands long time with mouth wide open waiting for roast duck to fly in."

The real reason they wouldn't believe was because they recognised that faith would necessitate radical changes in lifestyle. It was their wickedness that controlled their thinking.

Aldous Huxley was an avowed atheist author who wrote the great twentieth century dystopian novel 'Brave New World'. In his collection of essays, 'Ends and Means', he very honestly explained the rationale for his atheism. What he said is worth repeating,

"I had motives for not wanting the world to have a meaning; and consequently, assumed that it had none and was able without any difficulty to find satisfying reasons for this assumption. The philosopher who finds no meaning in the world is not concerned exclusively with a problem in pure metaphysics. **He is also concerned to prove that there is no valid reason why he personally should not do as he wants to do. For myself, as no doubt for most of my friends, the philosophy of meaninglessness was essentially an instrument of liberation from a certain system of morality. We objected to morality because it interfered with our sexual freedom.** The supporters of this system claimed that it embodied the meaning – the Christian meaning, they insisted – of the world. There was one admirably simple method of confuting these people and justifying ourselves in our erotic revolt: we would deny that the world had any meaning whatever."[112]

This is precisely what Jesus said, it is our determination to live our lives as we want that controlled how we assess evidence. Aldous Huxley had an open marriage and many mistresses!

A prominent American philosopher, Thomas Nagel, wrote a book called *The Last Word*. He had a deep dislike towards certain aspects of established religion – for what some people believe and do. However, he goes on:

"I want atheism to be true, and I am made uneasy by the fact that some of the most intelligent and well-informed people I know are religious believers. It isn't just that I don't believe in God and, naturally, hope that I'm right in my belief. It's that I hope there is no God! **I don't want there to be a God**; I don't want the universe to be like that. My guess is that this cosmic authority problem is not a rare condition. I am curious…whether there is anyone who is genuinely indifferent as to whether there is a God."[113]

The Sign of Jonah

Here in Luke's gospel the 'Sign of Jonah' was the fact that the evil city of Nineveh repented when they were challenged by Jonah's preaching – they repented and turned back to God. In the British museum, there are some carvings that portray the wickedness of the people of Nineveh. They would spear their enemies, chop off their legs, flay them alive and remove their heads!

The Ninevites were certainly a pagan, cruel, and utterly evil people yet they could repent wholeheartedly at the message of judgment! Jesus says that these men of Nineveh will stand up at the final day of judgment and condemn the Jews for not believing in the need for repentance, for turning back to God.

Jesus frequently compared the behaviour of the Jews, God's chosen people with that of outsiders and he then gave another example. If a foreigner, the Queen of Sheba, could recognise the wisdom of Solomon, could travel a very long way to ask him hard questions, could so learn about God, and could end up persuaded, then what is stopping the Jews, a more privileged people from discovering the

---

[112] Aldous Huxley, Ends and Means (New York, NY: Harper & Brothers Publishers, 1937), 270.
[113] Nagel T. 'The Last Word' cited in Keller T. 'Encounters with Jesus'. New York: Penguin, 2013:86

truth. Sheba was the combined region of Yemen and Ethiopia so the journey would not have been easy.

The message of Jesus remains the same today. Whatever our past, anyone can start a new life as one of God's people, empowered by His Spirit, to live lives for his glory. Jesus had already set his heart on going down to Jerusalem where he knew he would be arrested and killed by crucifixion. Yet he was determined to go through with all this so that he could be the Saviour of the world. He would be cut off from his Father so we could be reconciled with God – such love. He would rise from the dead to prove his claim to be the very Son of God.

We may not know everything, but we all know enough especially about ourselves to know that we need to be forgiven by God if we are to have any future with him.

The Light Is Not Hidden

The wicked may claim that they do not have enough light to see the truth but Jesus rejects this claim.

"No one lights a lamp and puts it in a place where it will be hidden, or under a bowl. Instead, they put it on its stand, so that those who come in may see the light. Your eye is the lamp of your body. When your eyes are healthy, your whole body also is full of light. But when they are unhealthy, your body also is full of darkness. **See to it, then, that the light within you is not darkness**. Therefore, if your whole body is full of light, and no part of it dark, it will be just as full of light as when a lamp shines its light on you." Luke 11:33–36

Jesus repeatedly claimed to be the light of the world that is not hidden.

To be in the dark is a miserable state to be in. We lack knowledge, we are outsiders, we cannot see the right way to go. When I was speaking at a student conference in Denmark, the organisers decided to take us all on a late-night walk through a local forest. It was totally pitch black, we couldn't see anything. The only way to move forwards was to hold onto the clothes of the person in front of you. It was eerie and most disorientating. When the military wants to break down a captive, it is common practice to place them in a pitch black cell as this tends to separate people from reality.

Jesus says that this is our natural spiritual condition. We are vulnerable and are liable to take the wrong paths. This light of God is available to all. This is why he is repeatedly described as 'a light to the Gentiles' (Isaiah 42:6, 49:6, Luke 2:32 and Acts 13:27). Jesus did what the Jews kept failing to do – to bring God's light to all people.

The suggestion that Jesus was hiding his light is bizarre. He deliberately went to Jerusalem so everyone could know about him and his sacrificial death. What is necessary is for people to go to where that light is,

"...so that those who come in may see the light." Luke 11:33

Culpability for not seeing the light remains on those who refuse to go to the light. Didn't Jesus say,

"Ask and it will be given to you; seek and you will find; knock and the door will be opened to you. For everyone who asks receives; the one who seeks finds; and to the one who knocks, the door will be opened." Matthew 7:7–8

I have just been watching some videos on YouTube of blind people who have been able to see after modern surgery. The thrill on their faces was wonderful – they can see after living in the dark for years. The same thrill is often experienced by those who come to see the light of Christ.

Why cannot everybody see how everything fits together in Jesus? The facts about him are clear. He explains why those innate instincts within all of us that life has a purpose, that there is right and wrong, that sin matters, that values such as honesty, courage and beauty are real. He gives those of us who are getting older both hope and security. It all makes sense but people do not want to see this.

At my medical school, I had a friend who asked me why I was a Christian. We spent a long time going over the evidence that had convinced me and he had no answers to the arguments. However, when I asked him whether he would be willing to commit himself to Christ he replied after a pause,

"No, I'm sorry but I see that it would mean great changes to the way I enjoy living now."

It was as if he had blinkers over his eyes, like a carthorse, and can only have a limited perspective.

The responsibility for seeking and obeying God's truth is ours. Jesus said,

"Blessed are those **who hear the word of God and obey it**." Luke 11:28

"**See to it then to see that the light within you is not darkness.**" Luke 11:35

If anyone wants to know whether what Jesus is saying about himself, they need to understand that the block is not in a lack of evidence about him, it is an unwillingness to obey what God has said. Elsewhere he said,

"Anyone who chooses to do the will of God will find out whether my teaching is of God." John 7:17

What will persuade people about Jesus?

No matter how hard we try or how many arguments we present, ultimately only God can persuade a person that the Gospel is both true and for them. Jesus said,

"No one can come to me unless the Father who sent me draws him." (John 6:44).

People are spiritually blind. I became a Christian because I saw that the Christians around me had something different about them that was admirable. They had a purpose and a morality that I instinctively knew to be right. It was the light in them that led me to look at their Jesus. Without seeing that difference, the arguments would have had much less impact.

This is why the most important thing we can do for our neighbours is to live good, godly lives and pray for them. Right now, they don't believe there is any need to have their sins forgiven – and therefore they don't believe they need Christ. They may think that they are relatively 'good' – but cannot see that in God's eyes they are rebels against his rule. Pray that they will face up to their own spiritual emptiness, and that God will convict them of their self-righteousness and need for Christ. The Bible says the Holy Spirit 'will convict the world of guilt in regard to sin and righteousness and judgment' (John 16:8).

Christians need to ask God to help us be a witness to others by the way we live – including the way we react when things don't go the way we wish they would. Anyone can be at peace when things are going well – but how do you react when things turn against you? The Bible says, 'But the fruit of the Spirit is love, joy, peace, patience, kindness, goodness' (Galatians 5:22). It is these interpersonal characteristics in us that make Jesus attractive and can lead them to respond to our invitations to investigate the truth of the claims of Christ, who alone can give hope for this life and the next.

Jesus wants all his people to be full of the light of the Spirit of Jesus in us. It is as if a spotlight is shining on us that others will see. Hidden sin in us will prevent this light shining. Jesus concluded,

"Therefore, if your whole body is full of light, and no part of it dark, it will be just as full of light as when a lamp shines its light on you." Luke 11:33

A student wrote to his tutor,

"I'm not coming back next term. I'm taking time out to find myself. I feel I am the product of what my family, society and school want me to be, but I want to get to the core of my being and find myself."

Such people seem to think they are like an onion and if only they can peel off the layers, the socially generated skins, they will find themselves at the core. Such thinking suggests that all of us have a true self waiting to be found. This is not true; self is something waiting to be created by what we commit ourselves to and live by.

This is why Jesus is both 'the sign of Jonah' and the 'lamp of the body,' he alone embodies intellectual truth and can give us a coherent satisfying experience of reality.

Chapter 20
Experience and Reason

Many people have found that their interest in Christ was initiated by an experience. Saul, later to be called Paul, was an ardent antagonist of the early church. He persecuted, imprisoned and attended the execution of those who had become followers of Jesus Christ. Then when he was travelling to Damascus to start a new scourge of Christians there, he had a life-changing experience.

As he neared Damascus on his journey, suddenly a light from heaven flashed around him. He fell to the ground and heard a voice say to him, "Saul, Saul, why do you persecute me?"

"Who are you, Lord?" Saul asked.

"I am Jesus, whom you are persecuting," he replied. "Now get up and go into the city, and you will be told what you must do." Acts 9:3

It was after this dramatic experience that Paul put everything together in his mind, yet this vivid experience remained a vital factor for the rest of his life. Many years later, when arrested in Jerusalem, he gave a detailed account of this experience to a massed crowd. He explained why he had changed direction and had become a Christian[114]. Again at his trial before King Agrippa II and Festus he repeats this story[115]. He then continued his defence by showing the King the Jewish Scriptures concerning God's Messiah that Jesus fulfils and in this way he supported the early experience he had had.

The God depicted in the Bible is not just an abstract philosophical idea but an all-powerful being with personality who is actively involved in his world. Although he is all powerful and able to do whatever he wishes, he has clearly chosen to allow this world to work according to rules he instituted. We call these

---

[114] Acts 21:40–22:22

[115] Acts 26:12–18

the 'Laws of Nature' though clearly nature itself cannot make rules, they should correctly be called 'Laws of God'. At times, especially when Jesus lived, these laws were suspended, and real miracles occurred. Outstanding examples of this is the resurrection of Jesus from the dead and the subsequent the gift of the Holy Spirit to all his church. This gift was a dramatic physical event associated with the sound of a violent wind, tongues of fire that separated to rest on each Christian and then the gift of courage so that they all started to tell those around them the facts about Jesus and they did this in the languages of visitors to Jerusalem, languages that they had never learned.

C.S. Lewis derided the idea that God can be trifled with or ignored with impunity when he wrote of Aslan, a model of Jesus,

'Safe?' said Mr Beaver; "Don't you hear what Mrs Beaver tells you? Who said anything about safe? Course he isn't safe. But he's good. He's the King, I tell you." [116] When God wants someone to belong to his people he acts. It is a basic doctrine in the Bible that God chooses those people who are to be his. We know we are one of the chosen people because we want to be forgiven, give up our independence and join others in God's church to be the ambassadors of Jesus Christ. He calls people who are both religious and irreligious but it is not until we enter into a personal relationship with Jesus Christ that we are secure or saved.

God calls us in a wide variety of ways, sometimes through experiences, sometimes through guilt and sometimes through logical conviction. It is an interesting finding that nearly all Christians can look back and see that God worked in their life through two factors – the presence of an obedient Godly Christian and an opening up to them of the Word of God.

C.S. Lewis' Story

C.S. Lewis was a brilliant scholar in Oxford. As an atheist he had many discussions with Christian friends such as J.R Tolkien, the author of 'the Hobbit' and 'Lord of the Rings' trilogy. The notion of God kept going round and round in his head. It was when he was on a bus going up Headington Hill in Oxford that he was suddenly struck with the idea that there must be a God. He had become a 'theist' but still not a Christian. He studied, read the Bible, and discussed much more now. The Bible became a major book of interest. It was

---

[116] C.S. Lewis, 'The Lion, the Witch, and the Wardrobe'

when he was on a journey coming back from Whipsnade Zoo that he came to the conclusion that Jesus Christ was God. There and then he committed his life to him. He described himself as 'the most reluctant convert in England'. Over the subsequent years he investigated all types of evidence, both objective, social and instinctive, and became one of the greatest apologists for the Christian faith. His books are still widely read and help many.

Augustine's Story. (354–430 AD)

Augustine was a bright but profligate youth. His mother was a Christian but he turned his back on her way of life. He had an illegitimate son but deep down he knew that there was a profound meaning to life. Augustine visited an aged and highly venerated priest in Milan called Simplicianus. Augustine told Simplicianus of his theological agonies, and Simplicianus replies by telling Augustine about Victorinus, a famous and erudite translator of Neoplatonic books, books that Augustine had recently been reading. Victorinus had become a Christian. This story deeply affected Augustine as Victorinus was highly educated. The fact that a man of such philosophical and intellectual prowess should turn to Christ made Augustine 'ardent to follow his [Victorinus'] example.' However, much he longed for peace with God he still could not find this.

One day he was under a fig tree weeping in a garden with a deep longing for peace when he heard a child in the next-door garden say repeatedly 'Tolle lege', 'Tolle lege', 'Take up and read', 'Take up and read'. He had never heard of a game with these words but as he had previously been reading from the Bible, he determined to follow the advice, thinking it was a message from God. Augustine wrote:

"So I quickly returned to the bench where Alypius was sitting, for there I had put down the apostle's book when I had left there. I snatched it up, opened it, and in silence read the paragraph on which my eyes first fell:"

"Not in rioting and drunkenness, not in chambering and wantonness, not in strife and envying, but put on the Lord Jesus Christ, and make no provision for the flesh to fulfil the lusts thereof."

I wanted to read no further, nor did I need to. For instantly, as the sentence ended, there was infused in my heart something like the light of full certainty and all the gloom of doubt vanished away.

"Not in riots and drunken parties, not in eroticism and indecencies, not in strife and rivalry, but put on the Lord Jesus Christ and make no provision for the flesh in its lusts." Rom 13:13–14 [117]

Thus began Augustine's Christian life. He was to become perhaps the greatest theologian the world has known. The inconsistent rough edges of his old life were put behind him. He now had a coherent world view that gave him peace and he determined to live for his Saviour.

The Rev William Haslam's Story

William Haslam had always been a religious man. He did his best to live as he thought God wanted him to. He was ordained and became a vicar in Cornwall, but he didn't know God. He became very troubled and another clergyman suggested that the real problem was that he had never relied on Christ for his salvation and challenged him whether he was truly born again. That Sunday morning he felt particularly low but thought that he ought to go to his church as there would be many coming. He decided that they would just sing a hymn and then he would send everyone home. However, as the hymn finished he decided to read the lesson which was from John chapter 6. When the reading finished, he thought he could give a short talk on this passage. However, as he was preaching he grasped for the first time that it was not what he did for God that mattered but what Christ had done for him. He was choked with a mixture of joy, peace and a new love for Christ. He later wrote of his experience. At the back of this book is a print showing a packed church with one of the congregations standing up and exclaiming, "The pastor is converted."

God remains the same and calls people today in all sorts of ways but still his Spirit usually works through obedient Christians who pass on the message of the Bible.

The following are the stories of two of my friends who became Christians through strange beginnings but these drew them to Christian friends and the Bible.

---

[117] Aurelius Augustine, 'The Confessions of St Augustine', book 8, chapter 12 para 29

Nick's Story

Nick is a very bright musician who had been brought up in a humanist home that had rejected God. At university, where he studied Chinese and Philosophy, he used to ridicule the Christians. Then something happened that was later to lead to a profound change in his life. He wrote,

"As a final year undergraduate, content in my modern, right-thinking humanist worldview I went to bed. Within a few minutes and still awake, I found myself in the presence of God. After just the briefest of meetings, the presence receded, and I again found myself wide awake but with a worldview that had just been smashed to pieces. Such Damascene conversions, like the Apostle Paul's in the first century are unusual and deeply personal. Thankfully, only some of us are so antagonistic to Jesus and thick-skinned as to need such an obvious and personal kick up the metaphorical backside. Most Christians come to a living faith through natural means alone: an open mind and the rational appeal of the gospel."

I am not so naïve as to expect anyone to believe my story of the supernatural at face value or think that it might have happened without scientific explanation. After all, it sounds rather absurd in our age, does it not, to say you met with the living God and that he spoke to you? With many years between then and now even I might be given to question its veracity; except that like an underwater earthquake it started a tsunami wave that is still running and which provides all the evidence I need to know it was for real.

A few days previously I had dominated the conversation amongst a group of friends where I had demolished the existence of God with my 'proofs', which were in fact just impressive sounding arguments of logic learned as a Philosophy student. A week later, the same group of friends found me strangely quiet when conversation returned to the subject again. Eventually being challenged to speak, I stated, as simply as I could, that I had changed my mind. I now knew that God existed although the details were well beyond my grasp. Do not underestimate the courage it takes for such a public admission and to lay yourself open to ridicule and incredulity – my friends who knew me were amazed as the look on their faces testified.

As for those details, in truth I knew that I had met with the Christian God but did nothing much about this revelation, and a fresh study of the Bible did not feature on my agenda. After having grown up at a time more traditional in its attitudes, and attended a school where we were familiarised with the Bible stories, I thought I knew it already. And for a young man in his twenties in the vibrant sexual liberation of the 1970s the moral implications of the Bible would be uncomfortable. The clinching reason for lack of progress was that I had been told to keep looking, and I selfishly interpreted that as an excuse to prevaricate. And so life continued much as before except I now utterly rejected that the universe was the happy chance of blind, irrational forces happening to come together in an inexplicable harmony, and was quick to state it was deliberately crafted by an all-seeing, intelligent designer.

By the late 1980s I had secured a good City trading job, was married to a wonderful lady, with two thoroughly talented and captivating children, home was comfortable, and two cars sat on the driveway. Worldly success was mine but inside there was a growing emptiness and disenchantment. Life struck me as a meaningless treadmill of days without direction. As colleagues sought solace in drink and outbound pursuits I continued to try and soberly make sense of things. It was now that a seeming coincidence of conversations about God over a couple of months made me angrily tell God to keep off my back. But he had other ideas; I was being told it was time to 'sort out Jesus'. Exactly who is he?

Several years later I was referred to see a surgeon and needed an operation. I was somewhat apprehensive, and the surgeon asked me,

"Do you have a faith that helps you at a time like this or aren't you sure about these things?"

I briefly mentioned how I had been an atheist but had had this strange experience of God whilst a student, but that I was still unclear. He then simply said,

"Perhaps this will be an opportunity to think these things through."

The operation went well and I got on well with the surgeon. However, as he was discharging me he said,

"Would you like to come and join a small group of us who meet to read the Bible each week in my home?"

Three weeks later I found myself, surprisingly, at a Bible study in the home of a Christian. There were people like me with lots of questions, some with impressive academic qualifications and positions of responsibility in their careers. Here was the opportunity to consider Jesus and his claim to be the God whom I had met. I found myself intellectually intrigued, but also challenged because the evidence in favour of Jesus being for real quickly overtook those against. Even the clever words of Richard Dawkins and his ilk could not prevail here.

At heart, the Christian truth is profoundly simple in that it starts and ends with a person – Jesus. But the depths of this truth will keep the human mind occupied for a lifetime. When he says, "I am the way, the truth and the life," he is saying he is the defining point of all things. He is the prime mover of the physical universe and all it contains, and he is the only true premise of all rational arguments about the reality of our lives. Like a visual illusion when you finally see it, the Christian gospel is so obviously right and true in every respect, describing the world and my life as it really is. Without Christ, the world remains an illusion and nothing that happens makes any sense or has any intrinsic value. No wonder that our young people, raised in a godless time, are so nihilistic.

Remember I was an affirmed atheist, but it is now my conviction that other atheists and humanists would come to say the same if they only stopped to let the Christ of the Bible speak to them too and to weigh the evidence with the same scale and measure they use for other matters. It is ironic that in order to deny God, the atheist knows exactly who the God is that has been denied. He nurtures an irrational inner anger towards him when the object of their anger is supposed not to exist! Furthermore, the atheist always speaks with precious little knowledge or understanding of the Bible and its doctrines and so gives away an ignorance as blind as those beloved memes and forces of chaos.

Dave's Story

"I have an unusual claim to fame – I believe I am the only person who has ever played in the national football Jewish and Christian Cup Finals!"

I was born to a typically east end Jewish family in 1952. My family weren't 'religious', but I went to Hebrew classes and believed in the God of Israel. I also proved to be one of the best Jewish footballers of my generation playing for Britain in the Maccabian Games in Israel and in several national cup finals.

However, after my bar mitzvah I pretty much ignored God for the next 25 years.

Then at the age of 38 in 1990, just like the queen, I experienced my 'Annus Horribilis'

In the space of 12 months I was divorced, lost custody of my two young children, was made redundant three times, lost my home and was left virtually penniless. Unsurprisingly this left me near suicidal and in an attempt to sort myself out I started to read the book *The Power of Positive Thinking*.

As I worked my way through the book, one Sunday evening I came across a chapter about praying directly to God – which as a Jew I had never really done before. I went to my room and prepared to pray. Suddenly and for no obvious reason I saw Jesus standing in front of me.

I know that sounds a little wacky when written in cold black and white, but it really happened and that one moment changed my whole life. Yes, me, a tough east end Jewish footballer, just like the apostle Paul, had received an appearance from the Lord Jesus himself.

And believe me it **was** Jesus (but don't ask me how I knew, I just did) and it **was** a vision (not a dream or something I had imagined). After initially feeling very frightened, I then had a warm feeling as if someone was putting their arm round my shoulder and telling me everything was going to be alright.

And how true that proved to be!

The next day I went into work and told my story to Steve – a new friend I had made who had told me that he had become a Christian. A remarkable series of what I thought then were 'coincidences' but I now know to be God's providences unfolded.

- Steve proceeded to present me with a new Bible that he had just purchased for me. I read the New Testament for the first time and found my heart strangely warmed and sensed that what I was reading was true.
- Steve said he and his church, which was many miles away in Thame Oxfordshire, were praying for me.
- Steve discussed my problems with a Christian at his church. It just so happened that the person Steve talked to had himself been helped to become a Christian through the friendship of someone at college who lived in Letchworth, North Hertfordshire, where I was now living. He suggested I phone this person whom he felt would help me. I did phone and was immediately invited round for a meal and a friendship and answers began to flow.
- My new friend encouraged me to join a course that he was just about to start, to look at the evidence of Jesus' claims to be the son of God, our Messiah, and what he taught.

- On this course, we were shown a video giving the testimony of Helen Shapiro, the retired pop star, and I realised that a Jew could become a Christian.

By the end of the course, I realised that the experience I had had with the vision of Jesus was supported by very good evidence that the claims of Jesus were true. I learned how I could be put right with God by the very Christ who had appeared to me. We read in the Bible what being one of God's people involves. I had no qualms about giving my life to God by asking Jesus to be my own Lord and Saviour.

And, oh, how my life changed from that point on. Spiritually, I found peace and purpose and meaning to my life. Materially, I got back into the job market and soon got back to a level of financial security. Emotionally, I met and subsequently married my beautiful wife, Heather, who had become a Christian at the very same time as me!

Even sportingly, at the age of 40, I started playing football again for a Christian team and got to the national Christian cup final to achieve that unusual claim to fame that I mentioned at the beginning.

It did take me a while to reconcile how you could be Jewish and Christian at the same time but the more I learnt about grace and that Christianity is not about a religion but a relationship with Jesus the more I came to terms with it. Of course, eventually I came to realise that I was in fact a 'complete Jew' and had great joy in going back to my Jewish roots and seeing the richness of my heritage of being one of God's chosen people.

I became a committed Christian, was baptised and was wonderfully mentored personally. When Heather and I moved to Chessington because of work, we soon became involved at the local Bible teaching church. I started to help with Christianity Explored courses and was involved in volunteering at the newly built Community Centre. I was soon asked to become a Deacon.

It seems as though God had a plan for my life that completely took me by surprise.

Such visionary experiences are uncommon and in any case experiences, visions and the like are never enough to substantiate an idea. They must be supported by reason and evidence. Jesus confirmed this when he was discussing with Jewish people his claim to be the Messiah, where he insists that the evidence is overwhelming.[118] New religions throughout the world have sprung up when people claimed they had received divine messages but their followers failed to verify the claims as Jesus did.

Most of us are attracted to Jesus when we see the Christian life being lived and then have the Christian message explained. Some are so attracted to Jesus and what they have seen in others and learned about him and his teaching that the intellectual questions are not an issue. Others want to have the 'i's' dotted and 't's' crossed before they make any decision about the place they will give to Christ in their life. What matters is not the route to faith but the change real faith brings. This is a major piece of evidence.

The Evidence Must Be Checked

One of the main reasons many are inclined to investigate the claims of Jesus is because of what we saw in some Christians lives. They did seem to have a friendliness, openness and integrity that was attractive.

'Sacred Hearts' was a film about some girls living in a Roman Catholic orphanage during the Second World War. One of the girls admitted to the rather austere nun in charge of her that she had lost her faith. She told the nun,

"I have lost my faith; I just started to think and I lost my faith."

To this the nun replied,

"Well, stop thinking and your faith will come back!"

What awful advice. If something is true, then it will always bear honest investigation. The girl should have been advised to weigh up all the evidence, evidence from science, evidence about Jesus and the evidence our instincts give us. Then she would see that the Christian story is true, really true, and that she can get right with God. The problem is that most people don't want to look at all the evidence because, deep down, they don't want God to be their God.

---

[118] John 5:31–47 and John 8:12–30

Chapter 21
'How Can I Be Saved?'

There is surely no greater question than 'How can I be saved?' yet how few people ask it. Many try to find salvation by membership of a church or organisation. They say, I'm an Anglican or I'm a Roman Catholic or Baptist, Methodist, Mormon, Jehovah's Witness, Jew or Muslim. These are the usual answers when people are asked about faith in proformas.

When I was visiting Indonesia, a young Muslim man explained to me that there were seventy-two separate groups within Islam and that only those in one of those groups were acceptable to God and would be saved. I asked him which group he was in.

"Oh, I'm in the group that are going to be saved!"

People think that because they belong to the organisation they are somehow 'protected'. However, membership of an organisation, however good its teaching, of itself cannot put anyone right with God. The Bible is clear that religious rites, such as circumcision, baptism, confirmation, communion, ordination or even consecration saves nobody. The Lord reminded the prophet Samuel,

" Man looks at the outward appearance, but the Lord looks at the heart." 1 Samuel 16:7

Similarly, he says to the church at Thyatira that God's judgment awaits those members of the church who do not live as he wants.

"Then all the churches will know that I am he who searches hearts and minds and I will repay you each according to your deeds." Revelation 2:23

In 1513, Pope Julius II died. He had achieved much, in material terms, for Rome. It was he who had the old St Peter's pulled down so he could build a much more impressive edifice. He was a powerful, arrogant, promiscuous and deceitful man constantly embroiled in warfare. Shortly after his death a pamphlet, 'Julius Excluded from Heaven', probably written by the great scholar Erasmus, was widely circulated and became very popular. It satirically describes what happens when a drunken Julius arrived at the gates of heaven and tries to open the gate with the key of his secret money chest. He is surrounded by the soldiers who have died in his military campaigns, whom he had promised admission to heaven, whatever they had done on earth. Peter refused him admission. Julius responds by threatening Peter with Bulls of Excommunication! Julius is described as the enemy of Christ, as a Julius Caesar returned from hell, and is accused of many vices which included drunkenness, pederasty, adultery and an obsession with money. He is contrasted with Jesus who, it claimed, is the true head of the church. The story finishes with Julius threatening to muster an army to capture heaven.

The Bible clearly teaches,

"For of this you can be sure: No immoral, impure or greedy person – such a man is an idolater – has any inheritance in the kingdom of Christ and of God. Let no-one deceive you with empty words, for because of such things God's wrath comes on those who are disobedient." Ephesians 5:5–6

In recent years, there have been innumerable stories of senior clergymen being actively involved in promiscuous relations with men, women and children. Clearly their cloth will not save them.

Who needs saving?

The unanimous verdict of both the Old and New Testaments is that there is nobody who is naturally good enough to stand in God's presence. King David confirmed what God saw in men.

"The Lord looks down from heaven on the sons of men to see if there are any who understand, any who seek God. **All have turned aside**, they have altogether become corrupt; **there is no-one who does good, not even one**." Psalm 14:2–3

God's decision about his own people in Isaiah's day (around 700 BC) was damning,

"But your iniquities have separated you from your God; **your sins have hidden his face from you**, so that he will not hear." Isaiah 59:2

The Bible teaches that sin is the fundamental problem of all mankind. Hardly a page can be read without this being stressed – it makes no difference whether a person is Jewish, religious or doesn't subscribe to any faith. Paul concluded,

"There is no difference, for **all have sinned** and fall short of the glory of God." Romans 3:23

How can we be saved?

We are in a desperate plight. We cannot save ourselves by what we do. The answer given in the Bible is that salvation is a gift, given only to those who have a personal relationship with Jesus Christ. The first ten verses of Paul's first letter to the troubled church at Corinth puts Jesus centre stage. Jesus is mentioned repeatedly. Similarly, the opening chapter of his letter to the Philippians leaves no doubt that his message is about Jesus Christ. Read the first few verses of his letter to the Colossians. It is not belonging to a church or organisation that saves anyone, it is living in a relationship with Christ that is the key to salvation. A local church will usually contain some who are saved as a result of their living in this relationship and some who are not. The key is to be 'in Christ' (Colossians 1:2). Paul doesn't commend them because of their membership of a church but for their submission to the Lord Jesus.

"…we have heard of your **faith in the Lord Jesus…**" Colossians 1:3

This is the message of the whole Bible and Paul stresses that it is from the Bible that people come to know the truth. The prime role of churches is to teach people what the Word of God is saying. Rituals are no substitute for this.

"…that you have already heard about in the word of truth, the gospel that has come to you." Colossians 1:5

The Christian 'good news' or 'gospel' is that anyone who enters into a personal relationship with Christ will be saved into eternity by him.

"**All over the world this gospel is bearing fruit and growing, just as it has been doing among you since the day you heard it and understood God's grace in all its truth.**" Colossians 1:6

Everybody needs to hear and have this message explained to them. This is what the Colossians needed.

"You learned it from Epaphras, our dear fellow servant, who is a faithful **minister of Christ** on our behalf…" Colossians 1:8

Note that Epaphras, who himself was a faithful minister of Christ, passed on the apostolic message; Paul says he was acting 'on our behalf'. To teach the precise message of the apostles is what true members of the 'holy, catholic, apostolic church' always do. We are simply channels of God's message.

To submit to Christ's rule and so accept the gift of salvation is only the beginning of a new life. Baptism, the initiatory rite, indicates that a person has died to the old life, that their sin has been washed away, and they have risen to live a new life for the Lord Jesus. Growth in the Christian life involves a growth in understanding and an increase in our determination to live effectively for Christ. This is why it is essential for all Christians to become involved with like-minded Christians who are also centred on living for Christ in the way his apostles make clear. God has given us his Scriptures to teach and encourage us and we neglect them at our peril. This is why Paul wrote his letters.

"…we have not stopped praying for you and asking God to fill you with **the knowledge of his will** through all spiritual wisdom and understanding. And we pray this in order that you may **live a life worthy of the Lord** and may please him in every way: bearing fruit in every good work, growing in the **knowledge of God**." Colossians 1:9–10

Every person who has entered into such a personal relationship with Christ is considered by God to be one of his holy people. We are all his 'saints'. Note how Paul uses this term repeatedly for all those 'in Christ'.

"…we have heard of your faith **in Christ Jesus** and of the love you have for all **the saints**." Colossians 1:4

"…giving thanks to the Father **who has qualified you** to share in the inheritance of **the saints in the kingdom of light**." Colossians 1:12

"…the mystery that has been kept hidden for ages and generations, but is now **disclosed to the saints**." Colossians 1:26.

It is a move away from apostolic teaching to just use the word 'saints' for those that the church considers 'distinguished'. God sees all people who are truly 'in Christ' as his sanctified, holy saints. Our standing does not come from ourselves but simply because we have been given our Saviour's righteousness through our relationship with him. Everyone in Christ's kingdom is given the status of being a saint because we have all been forgiven our sins because of and by Jesus.

"For **he has rescued us** from the dominion of darkness and brought us into the kingdom of the Son he loves, in whom we have redemption, **the forgiveness of sins**." Colossians 1:13–14

A patient of mine with terminal cancer had just become a Christian. She moved to the local hospice and I went to visited her there. She was holding firmly onto her Saviour even though she was unwell. We looked at a passage in the Bible that reassures us that all who are 'in Christ' are eternally secure. We read,

"Therefore there is **now** no condemnation for those who are in Christ Jesus..." Romans 8:1

To make this simpler to understand, I wrote her name on a piece of paper and placed this inside a closed Bible, saying,

"Let this Bible represent the Lord Jesus and this piece of paper represent you. Because you are now 'in Christ', God does not see your sins at all, he sees that you are in Christ and have 'his righteousness'. Furthermore Jesus has now gone to heaven and because you are in Christ he will take you to be with him there." Apparently, this meant a lot to her. A nurse told me later that she was asked to read the whole chapter of Romans 8 to the other patients in that unit.

Christians are now new people who are living for Christ. We are now members of the Kingdom of God. The only way to be acceptable to God is for us the be recognised as being 'holy', to be given this status as a free gift. This is only given to those who are 'in Christ'; they are 'credited' with Christ's righteousness (Romans 4:5), they are declared 'righteous' (Romans 3:20).

Why is Jesus so important?

Some readers may have been concerned at the way Paul puts Jesus at the centre of his message. A group of young people from another church came to one of our evening youth services and I went to welcome their leader. As I sat next to her, the first thing she said to me was,

"You people talk too much about Jesus!"

I tried to answer her by showing that this was really a compliment as the apostles did the same. We looked together at the beginning of Paul's first letter to the Corinthians. In the first ten verses, he keeps mentioning 'Christ Jesus', 'the Lord' and 'the Lord Jesus Christ'. The first chapter finishes with this reminder that Jesus Christ is everything to a Christian.

"Christ Jesus who has become for us our righteousness, holiness and redemption. Therefore, as it is written: let him who boasts boast in the Lord." 1 Corinthians 1:30–31

She couldn't see this. For her, the church should be focussing on remedying people's social and political needs.

It is not only Paul who focusses on Christ and the forgiveness all can find through him. When God spoke to Joseph to tell him that his fiancée, Mary, was about to have God's child he was told,

"You are to give him the name Jesus, because he will save **his people** from their sins." Matthew 1:21

The only people who will be forgiven their sins would be 'his people', Jesus' followers. Matthew then recalls the Old Testament prophecy about God's Messiah,

"The virgin shall be with child, and they will call him 'Immanuel' – which means, '**God with us**'." Matthew 1:23 and Isaiah 7:14

It is surely for this reason that the next section of Paul's letter to the Colossians emphasises who Jesus is and why this is so important. The only way anyone can be forgiven their sins is if God himself takes responsibility for our wrongdoings. If Jesus is not God we cannot be forgiven our sin – however:

"He is the image of the invisible God, the firstborn over all creation. For by him all things were created; things in heaven and earth, visible and invisible…he is before all things, and in him all things hold together…for God was pleased to have **all his fulness dwell in him**." Colossians 1:15–19

It is because he is the one and only Son of God that, by his dying on that cross, as our substitute he can pay for our sin and so reconcile us to God.

"…and through him to **reconcile to himself** all things…by making **peace through his blood shed on the cross**." Colossians 1:20

The apostle emphasises that this forgiveness and reconciliation is complete. We cannot become more holy in God's eyes than the Lord Jesus has made us through his death. This is thrilling news for those in Christ.

"But now he has reconciled you by Christ's physical body through death **to present you holy in his sight, without blemish and free from accusation…**" Colossians 1:22

Turning to Christ Is Only the Start

One evening Billy Graham, the twentieth century evangelist, was walking through a city when a drunkard, who was propping up a lamp-post, recognised him and called out,

"I'm one of your converts."

Billy Graham replied,

"That may be so, but you are clearly not one of Jesus Christ's converts."

There are unfortunately many who make a beginning to the Christian life with good intentions but who quickly turn away from him. A past experience of an emotional religious experience, of baptism or confirmation should just be the beginning of a life with Christ. Salvation is only found in Christ – leave him behind and we leave all hope of salvation. Paul continues the above sentence about our complete salvation,

"to present you holy in his sight, without blemish and free from accusation **if you continue in your faith, established and firm, not moved from the hope held out in the gospel**." Colossians 1:23

It does not say 'not moved from the church'. The New Testament is full of warnings that people may remain in the church institutions and yet drift from living with and for the Lord Jesus.

This gospel, that salvation is found when we are in Christ, is the universal or catholic gospel.

"This is the gospel that you heard and that has been proclaimed to every creature under heaven, and of which I, Paul have become a servant." Colossians 1:23

In an African primary school the children were set the task of composing and then reciting a poem about the Christian life. When it was his turn, a nine year old stood up and started his recitation,

"If you would be a Christian, go on, go on, go on, go on, go on, go on, go on…" – and so he continued!

Paul says very much the same later in this letter. It is not starting the race that counts, it is the finishing. We start this new life by individually turning to Christ as our King and our Saviour from sin. We continue as we daily spend our lives living to please him.

"So then, **just as you received Christ Jesus as Lord, continue to live in him**, rooted and built up in him, strengthened in the faith as you were taught, and overflowing with thankfulness." Colossians 2:6

A Costly Message

In March 2018, a twenty five year old radicalised Islamist went on the rampage in a supermarket in the south of France, killing three people and injuring sixteen others, two seriously. He then kidnapped a terrified woman and used her as a shield. At this point, a local policeman, Lt Col Arnaud, himself a committed Christian, offered himself in the woman's place. The exchange took place. The woman was released but Arnaud was stabbed and shot to death. Arnaud's brother said,

"He gave his life for strangers. He must have known that he didn't really have a chance. If that doesn't make him a hero, nothing does."

It cost Jesus his life to release us from sin and enable us to enter God's Kingdom. Paul had suffered much to ensure that this message became widely understood throughout the Roman world. He was eventually executed because of his determination to complete the task God had given him. This passion is what the next section in this letter describes. Nothing mattered so much to Paul as the passing on of the full message of God to Christ's people everywhere.

"I have become its servant by the commission God gave me to **present to you the word of God in its fullness** – the mystery that has been kept hidden for ages and generations but is now disclosed to the saints." Colossians 1:26

Paul cannot refrain from reminding us of what this message is,

"…to make known among the Gentiles the glorious riches of this mystery, which is **Christ in you, the hope of glory**." Colossians 1:27

The message is simple, it is all about who Christ is and what he came to do. It is clearly vital that everybody has the opportunity to both hear about and respond to this invitation of Jesus. Paul now moves away from talking about himself to describing the role of all Christians. Paul's life is just an example of how other members of God's church should live. We all need to tell others about who Christ is, what he has done for us and how we can be saved by entering into a relationship with him.

"**We proclaim him**, admonishing and teaching everyone with all wisdom, so that **we may present everyone perfect in Christ**. To this end I labour, struggling with all **his** energy, which so powerfully works in me." Colossians 1:28–29

This perfection can only be Christ's righteousness that has been given to his people.

Christianity Is Christ

W H Griffith Thomas wrote a classic Christian book entitled *Christianity is Christ*. In this he wrote,

"Christianity is the only religion in the world which rests on the Person of its Founder. A man can be a faithful Mohammedan without in the least concerning himself with the person of Mohammed. So also a man can be a true and faithful Buddhist without knowing anything whatever about Buddha. It is quite different with Christianity. Christianity is so inextricably bound up with Christ that our view of the Person of Christ involves and determines our view of Christianity.

The relation of Jesus Christ to Christianity differs entirely from that of all other founders towards the religions or philosophies which bear their names. Platonism, for example, may be defined as a method of philosophic thought from Plato; Mohammedanism as the belief in the revelation vouchsafed to Mohammed; Buddhism as the following of principles enunciated by Buddha. But Christianity is in essence adherence to the Person of Jesus Christ.

It has also been pointed out that Christianity alone of the great religions of the world calls itself by the name of its Founder, and that while we call other religions by the names of their founders, the adherents of these religions do not call themselves by these names. This fact is full of very deep meaning."

A Christian is devoted to Jesus Christ, is deeply grateful to him for the salvation he won for him or her on that cross and now lives to please him in the company of other followers of Christ.

For life to make sense, we must begin with God.

Summary

Philip Pulman, an ardent atheist, wrote a trilogy of books called *His Dark Materials,* the Magisterium wanted to control the thinking of people – ostensibly for their good. In the first of the films based of these books *The Explorer,* Lord Asriel Belacqua had come across the body of an explorer, Grumman, that the Magisterium had killed because he had discovered truths the Magisterium wanted to keep secret. When speaking to members of Jordan College in Oxford, Asriel explained his ideas that the Magisterium considered heretical. He said,

"The Magisterium is trying to keep us safely innocent or, as the Master would have it, academically free. There is a war waging right now, trying to keep us in ignorance and people like Grumman, willing to fight for the light, fight for truth, for academic freedom."

Asriel went on to say,

"I don't trust anyone."

To live without trust is a hard place to be in. The question we need to answer is which side is right, who is telling the truth. Is Jesus really the light of the world or are those who deny that there are real answers really following all the evidence that is available to us. This evidence of the *Stepping Stones* can be found both objectively, from science and rational thinking and subjectively from our inherent instincts about what matters in life. We have to make up our minds. As Joshua said to the Israelites shortly before he died,

"Choose for yourselves this day whom you will serve…" Joshua 24:15

We all serve somebody or something. If it is not our creator who has revealed himself in Christ it is usually ourselves or our interests. Many today simply accept that they live in this selfish and often worrying world yet go along with this world view. Yet there are indications that there is more meaning to life than just living in a way that satisfies us for a few years. Nearly everyone recognises that honesty, self-control and love are real values and that these are essential for living in families and in societies. Are these values a genuine part of our makeup or are they artificial standards imposed on us. There are also objective truths about this world that cannot be explained without there being a mind behind our existence. Science does require a mind to explain our design, the Laws of Nature, our DNA and our biochemical makeup. There are other indicators or 'Stepping Stones' that point to there being real answers to the meaning to life.

Then there is the person, life and death of Jesus who claimed to be the very Son of God, who does fulfil those old prophecies, who did extraordinary miracles and who finally became the ultimate sacrifice for sin before rising from the dead. The evidence for the resurrection is extremely strong and could never be overturned in a court of law.

The Bible does resonate with the values and purpose that people instinctively know to be true. If we are honest, we know that our standards are well below those of Jesus and when we die we will be guilty before him.

Yet the great news is that our creator really has stepped into our world to give us the solution we all need. The step of faith God requires is for us to accept God's rule in our lives and live by what Jesus, the Christ, God's Son and Chosen King, has taught us. This is not blind faith but reasoned faith based on the objective and subjective evidence. A blind leap of faith is to jump back to the selfish bank of the river without being bothered to answer all the evidence of each of the Stepping Stones. The Bible says that it is because man deliberately rejects God's rule that we will be held accountable to him at our judgment before him. The remedy is clear. Peter said to those who had rejected Jesus but felt bad about this,

"Repent and be baptised, everyone of you, in the name of Jesus Christ for the forgiveness of your sins. And you will receive the gift of the Holy Spirit." Acts 2:38

Hope is always available.